MY OWN
WORST ENEMY

Donna Kaye Laughlin

OTHER BOOKS BY ALAN NELSON

MY OWN WORST ENEMY

Overcoming Nineteen Ways We Defeat Ourselves

ALAN NELSON

FOREWORD BY JOHN C. MAXWELL

Fleming H. Revell
A Division of Baker Book House Co
Grand Rapids, Michigan 49516

Published by Fleming H. Revell
a division of Baker Book House Company
P.O. Box 6287, Grand Rapids, MI 49516-6287

Printed in the United States of America

Library of Congress Cataloging-in-Publication Data

Nelson, Alan, 1958-
    My own worst enemy : overcoming nineteen ways we defeat
ourselves / Alan Nelson ; foreword by John C. Maxwell.
        p.   cm.
    ISBN 0-8007-5791-2 (pbk.)
    1. Christian life. 2. Conduct of life. I. Title
    BV4501.3 .N45 2001
    158.1—dc21   2001048550

For current information about all releases from Baker Book House, visit our web site:

http://www.bakerbooks.com

This book is dedicated to the many mentors I've known, who have honed my life and helped me confront self-defeating behaviors. I've found that the life-sharpening influences of mentors and accountability groups are priceless for personal growth.

Dad and Mom
Grandma Nelson
Bill Ellwanger
Ray Ortlund
John Maxwell
Nancy, Jeff, Josh, and Jesse

Our pastors in covenant group:
Mark, Cal, Gary, John, Mark, Phil, and Keith

And our SFC staff:
Jonathan, Johnna, Mike, Deanna, Shari, Marti, Jenny, Penny, Amy, Kim, Lenoir, and Nancy

A man's own folly ruins his life, yet his heart rages against the LORD.

Proverbs 19:3

The wise woman builds her house, but with her own hands the foolish one tears hers down.

Proverbs 14:1

We've seen the enemy; and the enemy is us.

Author unknown

CONTENTS

FOREWORD

My friend Alan Nelson has provided one of the most insightful looks into the human soul and psyche that I've seen. The reason that so many of us blame our failures, problems, and shortcomings on others is that we're unwilling to probe deeper for the answers. Like the fairy tale suggests, the "mirror, mirror on the wall" shows us the face of our enemy. The big bad wolf is not so much huffing and puffing at our door as he is sabotaging us from the inside out. In my decades of ministry as a pastor and now as an author, speaker, and leadership developer, I'm convinced that we defeat ourselves far more than we are defeated by external circumstances. All too often we're tempted to blame others, when we have ourselves to fault.

As Alan will show you, with a little insight and intention, you can improve your lot in life considerably. The first step is in determining the main source of your failures. You'll find a pot full of golden wisdom and practical ideas for avoiding the many ways that we are our own worst enemies. This is a must read for anyone who is determined to reach his or her potential in life. I heartily recommend it.

John C. Maxwell
Founder of The INJOY Group
www.injoy.com

INTRODUCTION

As a kid, I picked up the game of tennis when my dad taught me at the town courts on his occasional days off. When we moved to Creston, Iowa, I hit against the practice wall nearly every day. Even when it was snowing, I'd be on the courts, practicing serves. By ninth grade, I could keep pace with the seniors and became the only freshman on the varsity tennis team. I was so proud. The fact that Creston had only eight thousand people in the whole town did little to dampen my enthusiasm. My love for the sport continued so that when we moved to a larger city, I continued to improve, vacillating between being the first- and second-place singles man.

For a while, my dreams of grandeur drove me to think about becoming a pro. I had only one problem. I did not consistently win. Time after time, the same guy would defeat me—me. When I needed a point most, I'd commit unforced errors—double faults, overheads into the net, wide or long shots. Sometimes I'd even squander a commanding lead of 5 games to 1, only to lose the set. My primary foe on the court was not the opponent on the other side of the net; it was me. I was my own worst enemy.

After my professional tennis fantasy dissipated, I prepared for the ministry. Pastors have a unique job. They have the opportunity and responsibility to work with people through their highest and lowest times. On any given day of the week, I might perform a wedding, go to the hospital to celebrate the birth of a child, conduct a funeral, and counsel a couple going through divorce or personal trauma.

I remember a two-day period following the aftermath of the Oklahoma City bombing when I assisted three families who had learned that their loved ones had been killed, then drove to my office to counsel a couple pondering divorce, another planning a marriage, and a third who was celebrating a new birth. The hot/cold, up/down, high/low situations at times approach schizophrenic dimensions.

Through years of pastoring, you learn a lot about human nature, our decision-making process, and the consequences and chain events resulting from these decisions. Unlike professional counselors who tend to delve deeply into a few clients' lives each year, the pastor of a large or growing church will hear the stories of hundreds of lives annually. Consistent themes come to light. After staring at a 3-D poster, suddenly the hidden patterns emerge from the two-dimensional print. Similarly, after two decades of staring at numbers of people and their problems, common patterns emerge. By far, a majority of the frustrations, challenges, and failures in life are not the result of outside forces bent on our destruction. Unfortunately they are caused by our own responses.

The temptation is to blame other people and circumstances for our undoing. We point fingers at spouses, ex-spouses, parents, bosses, employees, siblings, birth order, ethnicity, pastors, God, government, corporations, and dumb luck. The blame game must be our favorite pastime. "Pass the Buck" should be our national anthem. But behind the visible circumstances is the less than obvious reality that most of us are our own worst enemy. Our number one nemesis is staring back at us in the mirror.

You may say, "Ah, but that's not me. You don't know my situation. I'm a victim of others who are out to put me down, plus unfortunate and vanished opportunities." Perhaps, but more commonly our downfall is what I call the bad choice chain reaction. Let's say a concrete truck's brakes fail and the behemoth plows into the back of a car at an intersection. This car in turn hits a pickup, and the pickup rams another car, which hits another, which hits another. Every rear-ended driver can look in his mirror and see the vehicle that hit him. He can point a finger and rightly identify the damage maker as the one closest to his back bumper. Right? Yes and no. The instigator of the chain of fender benders was the concrete-truck driver. While many of us point at the apparent offender in our lives, we quite often overlook the primary instigator—ourselves.

If the Pareto principle (80/20 rule) holds true here, we could assume that 80 percent of the problems, failures, and frustrations we endure in life are self-induced. Thus if there was some way to identify and address these self-sabotaging behaviors and attitudes, we would naturally improve our success, fulfillment, and productivity. Instead of focusing 80 percent of our attention on the 20 percent of legitimate problems not under our control, it would make sense to pinpoint how we are indulging in self-sabotage and strive to change our habits.

If you're my age, you may remember the old *Dick VanDyke Show*. Each week Dick came home to a house full of friends and tripped over the footstool. As a child, I could not figure out why he didn't just move it. But we're a lot like Dick. Time and again we trip over the same obstacles that litter our lives.

My Own Worst Enemy deals with the nineteen most common ways people sabotage themselves. I refer to these as "behavitudes." *A behavitude is a behavior that emanates out of an attitude.* Although some attitudes are created and primarily motivated by actions and behaviors, I've discovered that 80 percent of our behaviors are attitudinally based. In other words, you can change a behavior temporarily, but unless you also transform the attitude, you'll see its fruit popping up again. Our behaviors are often the things that get us into trouble, but most of them are attitude generated. Because it's sometimes difficult to determine the cause of our undoing—whether it is behavioral or attitudinal—I prefer the behavitude concept, which encompasses both. Someone said, "You cannot travel inside without moving outside," meaning that inner change ultimately results in external behavior.

I've noticed that it is easier to see the piece of spinach stuck in my wife's teeth than it is to see something stuck in my own. What is true about teeth is also true of weaknesses. We're often blind to our own faults. Perhaps the archenemy of us all is denial. We try to avoid responsibility and negative introspection at all costs. The temptation to put the blame on others and on external circumstances is huge. Many fall into this sin, suggesting that they are victims of some invisible conspiracy. "God is out to get me." "I had a harsh potty training." "I'm a middle child." "I'm from a dysfunctional family." The list is endless. Perhaps we should create a special web site for up-and-coming legitimate-sounding reasons for failure and frustration: www.excuses.com. In the movie *The Kid*, Bruce Willis's character responds to such whining with, "Somebody call a waaaaaaaaaaaaaaaambulance." Want a little cheese to go with that whine?

But when it's your pain, it's no laughing matter. Most of us feel justified in complaining when we feel life has done us wrong. This usually demonstrates our unwillingness to search for blame within ourselves.

As you read through the nineteen behavitudes, some will sound familiar. Faces will begin popping up in your mind, people who clearly err in one or more of these self-defeating patterns. Unfortunately it's more difficult to see the behavitudes in ourselves. The honest, motivated reader will not only contemplate which of the nineteen pertain to him or her, but may also want to seek the loving insight of a friend or family member for verification. People tend to see us differently than we see ourselves. We are often each other's best consultant and sometimes our own worst one.

In order to structure a look at these behavitudes, I've chosen the following template for each chapter: Each of the following chapters deals with one behavitude. I discuss how the behavitude can be detrimental and why people still indulge in it. Then I give four solutions to overcoming the behavitude. At the end of each chapter is a self-assessment, five questions for you to answer. They will help you estimate your involvement in this behavitude. Finally there are discussion questions that will guide groups and individuals in determining what they need to do to apply the ideas of the chapter.

You can use this book as a self-help course. If you're brave you may want to ask a close relative or friend to answer the questions with you in mind. You'll be able to look at the score they give and see whether or not you may be defeating yourself via the behavitude described. This book can also be used in group discussions and may be a great gift to send, without a return address, to someone you know who exhibits some of these self-defeating characteristics.

Throughout the book, I'll illustrate the problems and solutions with contemporary stories as well as biblical examples. I use the Bible in part because it is familiar fodder, since I am a pastor. I use it also because the Bible is the most respected book ever written, and you'll see that many of these behavitudes are enduring human challenges, not just modern or faddish faults. A final reason I use biblical principles for direction is because of the incredible interest in spirituality these days. Our Creator endowed us with free will. Whether you buy into the Scriptures or not is your own prerogative, as is your choice of sabotaging yourself through negative behavitudes. My hope is that you will be open to the truths of the Bible that millions have discovered throughout history as transformational, and that through this book you will grow in your relationship with your Creator.

The behavitudes in this book can be tied to deeper, spiritual conditions and consequences that enhance or retard our spiritual growth. This interests me because soul growth is my business, my profession. It is my prayer that as you read this book, you will come to grips with the behavitudes that are holding you back from reaching your greatest potential. Unlike some popular philosophies, this book does not suggest that the answer is within you. The problem, on the other hand, is a different matter.

one

SPILLED MILK

"Ohhhhh, I blew it," the woman groaned. "I messed up royally."

"How did you mess up?" I asked.

"When I left my husband ten years ago."

"Why did you leave him?"

"Oh, you know. We just weren't getting along well. He was a bit too controlling and couldn't give the level of care I wanted. He said I was a nag and he made negative comments about my body at times. That burned me up. Of course, I wasn't perfect either," she admitted.

"So don't you think you could have worked things out?" I asked.

"Maybe, but after I left, he wanted a divorce. Then he moved away and remarried. We were young, a bit impulsive, and I jumped to conclusions. I've not been able to get involved in a serious relationship since Jon, because I feel so bad and I don't want to make the same mistake again."

Description and Dangers

"Regrets, I've had a few," the song confesses. Most of us, if we're honest with ourselves, could come up with a boatload of mistakes we've made, people we've hurt, and opportunities we've blown. While taking responsibility for our errors is important, one very popular self-sabotaging behavitude is choosing to stay in unhealthy guilt instead of cleaning up the mess.

Did your mother ever tell you not to cry over spilled milk? She meant that what's done is done. Crying over it won't change what happened. She didn't mean, however, that you shouldn't clean up the milk you spilled.

Healthy guilt is an emotional or mental conviction that results in a behavioral change. Unhealthy guilt is when we stay locked into our sense of failure, are unable to act on it, and are unable to move on. People with unhealthy guilt feel the need to be punished. Recently a successful businessman informed me he was leaving our church. He said, "I need to get hit over the head every Sunday." "Head hitting" is usually a felt need among those who for one reason or another want to feed a guilt complex. Weekly church beatings serve as emotional floggings, the punishment some people believe they deserve. Guilt is a very difficult form of self-sabotage from which to disengage.

Related to unhealthy guilt is debilitating regret. Those who can't let go of their own or others' past mistakes may find themselves immersed in regret.

Forgiveness is the key to getting beyond guilt and regret. We must learn to forgive ourselves and others when milk has been spilled. This is needed when we spill our milk, when others spill our milk, and when we spill others' milk. The first has to do with times we've failed ourselves—breaking a New Year's resolution, vowing to stay clear of another person, saying yes to that extra helping of food, entertaining lustful thoughts, and putting off exercise. Examples of others spilling our milk are legion. Being rude to us, gossiping about us, breaking a promise, cutting us off in traffic, insulting us, and physically abusing us are some examples. When we do these things to other people, we're spilling their milk.

Spilled milk, in the context we're using the phrase, pertains to any number of past events where guilt, failure, and others' offenses become the focal point of our present lives. This in turn hampers our future health and well-being because we're fixated around something that cannot be undone. The majority of this section will look at how we deal with our own guilt.

Do you have the following symptoms of being stuck in guilt or regret?

1. You have a gnawing sense of guilt, conviction, and remorse.
2. You are condemning, critical, or self-righteous toward others.
3. You often demonstrate self-flagellation and false humility regarding your unworthiness.

The Danger of Exaggerated Damage

An active guilt complex tends to overly dramatize the harm done. For example, a woman says something unkind about a work associate. She feels so bad about the rude comment that she avoids the associate for days. She suffers from headaches and cannot concentrate on her work because of what she said.

The inverse of exaggerated guilt is exaggerated offense, when someone has injured us. Instead of letting a stray comment or criticism fade as so much noise, we invent all sorts of retaliatory maneuvers. When we replay the episode over and over, the perceived damage grows in intensity. Huge conflicts are often created out of minor altercations.

The Danger of Blaming to Avoid Guilt

Sometimes we find relief from the guilt we feel by putting the blame on others or on circumstances. No one enjoys admitting personal inadequacies or failures, so we avoid it by keeping the focus off our participation. "I only drove the getaway car. I was the helpless victim of the situation, taken hostage by the moment."

By blaming other people for our failures or drawing attention to the factors surrounding our sins, we play down our responsibility for what happened. This is self-defeating because it convinces us that we are victims of powers greater than ourselves, which in turn affects our self-esteem and sense of security.

The Danger of Unhealthy Anger

Another common response to guilt is anger. Not all angry people are suffering from unhealthy guilt, but anger is common because it is defensive in nature. The guilt-ridden person feels accused, condemned, and cornered. The natural response is to defend himself against perceived attack. The husband who has been lusting profusely or involved in an affair becomes critical of his wife for little reason. The woman who feels guilt-ridden for gossiping and maligning a friend's reputation treats the victim as her enemy.

The slow burn of guilt tends to corrupt our relationships with people who are unrelated to our failure. The damaged soul is akin to an injured animal that lashes out at helping hands. We confuse those who draw near to us with those who would take advantage of us in our weakened condition, and we respond to them in anger.

The Danger of People-Pleasing

Another response to the unhealthy behavitude of holding onto guilt is the groveling, self-demeaning attitude of a people-pleaser. As a means of working off his or her emotional debt, a person chooses to behave like a human doormat, inviting others to take advantage of him or her. "Go ahead, abuse me. Use me. I'm a worthless soul for all the bad I've done." Often there are people willing to comply.

Although the people-pleaser may appear outwardly to be a dedicated servant, his or her acts of service are not done out of a sincere desire to help others. Guilt-ridden people may appear to be the most subservient, submissive, humble people you will meet. And they are often mistakenly esteemed as saints within communities that value such traits as humility and service. Guilt-ridden servanthood, however, is not service from a humble heart but rather an attempt of the people-pleaser to assuage his or her guilt.

Crying over Spilled Milk

In an ideal world, guilt serves as a healthy indicator to remind us when we have erred ethically, morally, or socially. It pricks our soul so that we do not repeat the act or harm ourselves or others even further. Just as pain receptors tell us when our skin is being cut by a knife, when our finger is on a hot stove, or when we're pushing the exercise to the point of harm, guilt is designed to warn our souls of impending danger. It says, "Stop. Go back. Don't do this again. Correct the situation. You've done something damaging."

Because we're moral beings, we sense guilt. Immoral beings do not feel guilt. Just as a broken fuel gauge does not give you a proper reading of how much gas is in your tank, a disconnected conscience often results in all sorts of faulty soul readings. But just as a malfunctioning gauge can indicate more gas than is present, an overly active conscience creates inordinate guilt feelings that hinder our well-being.

Why do we cry over spilled milk if it is self-defeating? Here are four reasons:

1. *Crying over spilled milk provides us with a sense of penance.* It is a way that we try to forgive ourselves and/or earn another chance. Since we feel powerless about

unspilling the milk, feeling guilty is a form of emotional punishment and may ease our conscience for a time. It is an attempt to buy forgiveness through self-flagellation.

2. *The past, even if bad, is more secure than an unknown future.* By focusing on the spilled milk, we can avoid cleaning it up, driving to the store to buy more milk, or replacing our neighbor's milk that we spilled. We avoid moving on. Going forward can be scary. The effort to move ahead is often painful. Thus we live in the spilled milk instead of wiping it up and progressing. Living in the past is a self-sabotaging behavitude, but when we live there among our own broken promises and lapses, the harm is multiplied. Growth requires cleaning up the mess we made and setting out to pursue new goals.

3. *We are socially conditioned to feel shame.* Depending on our upbringing, some of us can manufacture guilt at the drop of a hat. We shame ourselves before others do in an attempt to save face. This knee-jerk reaction is often a conditioned response more than it is a conscious, intentional choice.

In the past, churches have cornered the market on guilt production, not to mention attracting guilt-ridden people. Certain congregations and associations of churches have taken advantage of this self-sabotaging response. Many of these religious organizations both create and feed off people with this behavitude instead of relieving it. They want to improve giving, attending, and serving, and they use guilt to do it.

Shaming is one of the strongest manipulative tools. Guilty people, by shaming themselves sufficiently, can actually gain sympathy from those they injure. How's that for a twist on reality?

4. *We fail to understand a healthy spiritual response to guilt and remorse.* Our emotional responses are often cre-

ated by faulty thought processes. Nearly all unhealthy guilt feelings can be traced back to "should" statements. "I should have done that." "I should not have done that." While "de-shoulding" our self-talk is a very effective, therapeutic solution, sometimes it is insufficient by itself.

Becoming Your Own Best Ally

Accept Your Limitation to Self-forgive

The nonbiblical means of coping with this guilt problem is to try to forgive yourself. The world says, "Forgive yourself. Let it go. Don't feel bad about past failures." Of course, if you are innocent of a failure, there is nothing to forgive. If you are at least in part guilty of some wrongdoing, then forgiving yourself is akin to lifting yourself off the ground by pulling on your socks. You do not have a foundation from which to leverage your forgiveness.

Self-forgiveness is different from accepting forgiveness. For justice to be served, someone must pay the price for the wrongdoing. When you get a traffic ticket, for example, you cannot legally tear it up. Only a judge can forgive you. This is why I find a biblical explanation most effective. It explains how we can receive forgiveness for wrongdoing:

> My dear children, I write this to you so that you will not sin. But if anybody does sin, we have one who speaks to the Father in our defense—Jesus Christ, the Righteous One. He is the atoning sacrifice for our sins, and not only for ours but also for the sins of the whole world.
>
> 1 John 2:1–2

If we claim to be without sin, we deceive ourselves and the truth is not in us. If we confess our sins, he is faithful and just and will forgive us our sins and purify us from all unrighteousness.

1 John 1:8–9

The warning applies, "Don't attempt this at home." Let God, the professional, handle forgiveness.

Pursue God's Forgiveness

Self-forgiveness is unreasonable because we do not have the authority to undo our sins or moral and ethical failures. Creating our own moral cleansing plan is different from accepting one that God, the ultimate judge, provides. His plan involved sending his only Son, Jesus, the perfect being, to die as a means to pay the price of our sins—past, present, and future. I'm not fully sure how or why this antidote works. No matter how deeply theological we get, the process requires faith. Even though a pharmacist can describe the chemical reaction between the drug and the body, still the patient must take the medication to experience the anticipated result. That is faith, an action based on a belief without full proof.

Holistic Forgiveness

The forgiveness prescription involves four steps: confession, repentance, restitution, and acceptance.

1. *Confession* comes first, because it acknowledges ownership. "I did it. I'm the one. Look no further to find the person to blame. I'm busted." By owning your mistakes, you can effect change. But confession alone is insufficient to do this. It must be accompanied by repentance.
2. *Repentance* has to do with having a "change of mind," the literal translation of the word. When a person

changes in mind, attitude, and heart, he or she heads in a different direction. Confession without repentance demonstrates responsibility with no intent to respond differently in the future. Guilt without repentance is anger at being caught.

3. The third step is *restitution*. This is when your attitude produces action. You replace the loss as best you can. You apologize and prove your remorse in some tangible way.

   Without confession and repentance, restitution is a means of self-forgiveness. It assumes you can redeem yourself by buying down the debt. This is what big companies often do. They make legal or fiscal restitution without admitting guilt, which is a frustrating, inhuman approach to making things right.

   For true restitution to take place, it must follow the confession of wrongdoing and repentance. Because talk is cheap, it is only after our appropriate inner response that our outward behavior gains value.

   Do your best to make things right. If it is impossible, move on directly to step four.

4. Next, we *accept forgiveness*. For many of us with a sensitive conscience, being forgiven induces another round of guilt. We feel as though we shouldn't be let off so easily. Accepting forgiveness, however, is not the same as lowering or desecrating standards. Unpacking forgiveness rightly does not make a mockery of justice. It merely recognizes that the price of your sin was too high for you to pay. You must therefore rely on God's grace. Jesus demonstrated the precarious balance of justice and grace. He had the uncanny ability to be both conservative in his values and liberal in his methodologies. He did not condemn the woman caught in adultery, but he warned her to "go and sin no more." As this woman discovered, being forgiven is an honor and an undeserved

privilege. When we understand the cost of forgiveness, we will have a corresponding attitude of humility and graciousness.

Intentional Forgetfulness

Unlike confession and even repentance, accepting forgiveness usually requires ongoing maintenance. The problem is one of memory. We all have mental VCRs in which we rerun past, multisensory events of our spilling milk. In the movie *Men in Black* the government agents had a top secret memory-inhibiting device. Unfortunately, that device is only fiction. We've not developed a drug that will erase our memory banks of past failures.

For forgiveness to retain its effectiveness, we must keep reminding ourselves of it, long after the behavior has been committed and the forgiveness received.

Forgiveness is both an action and an attitude (a behavitude) on the parts of the offended and the guilty persons. The act of forgiveness must often be followed up with a series of forgiving attitudes. Our minds play subtle tricks on us. We involuntarily replay the failure tape, time after time after time. Sometimes, the thought of the other person or a circumstance similar to the one surrounding the wrongdoing can act as a stimulus to engage the memory tapes. When this happens, we must remind ourselves of the forgiveness we have received.

SELF-SABOTAGE ASSESSMENT

Place a value of 1 to 5 in the box beside each statement: 1 = no/rarely 2 = infrequently 3 = sometimes 4 = usually 5 = yes/always

☐ 1. I forget past sins and errors I've committed.
☐ 2. I am able to forgive others regardless of their remorse because I've received forgiveness for my faults.
☐ 3. I avoid criticizing and condemning others because I realize my need for grace as well.
☐ 4. I anticipate the future, realizing that past failures need not ruin tomorrow.
☐ 5. I realize I cannot forgive myself but can accept God's forgiveness.

Add the numbers and divide by 5. If your score is 1–2.5, you are probably being an enemy to yourself in this area. If your score is 2.6–3.75, you may want to consider this area more to see what is fuzzy or what you could do to improve it. If your score is over 3.75, you are either strong in this area or partially blind, which may require a perspective of someone who knows you well.

Self-sabotage assessment: _____

Another person's assessment of me: _____

UNPACKING PROCEDURES

1. Describe a time when you lamented greatly over a spilled-milk episode.
2. What are some ways you notice that you or others try to unspill the milk by doing penance?
3. Think of a time when someone else displayed very little remorse for his or her offense. What seems

to be the right balance between healthy restitution or remorse and unhealthy self-flagellation?

4. What is one thing you would do over in your past if you could?

5. How would this "do-over" change your present or future?

6. Can you think of anyone you know who sabotages himself or herself by crying over spilled milk? How would you advise this person?

two

I CAN'T SAY YES

Phil confessed his frustrations to me.

"Shari just can't commit to anything. We've been engaged for over a year and now she's telling me that she's not ready to get married. She's been engaged two previous times as well. Our relationship is great. She's such a sweet, beautiful woman, but getting her to make a big decision is next to impossible. I feel like I'm living out the movie *Runaway Bride*."

Shari rarely stayed in a job more than a couple of years, feeling the need to look for greener grass. Each time she changed jobs, though, she made a lateral move instead of moving up. When you talk to her, she tells you convincingly how she came to her conclusions, but after a while, you get the feeling that she's afraid of making long-term commitments.

Two years later, Phil married another woman. When they are being honest, both Phil and Shari admit that they wish their relationship had worked out, but Shari just would not say yes.

Description and Dangers

Later in the book, we'll address the problem plaguing many of us, the seeming inability to say no to the wrong things. But the overlooked counterpart that sabotages us is the inability to say yes to the right things. Counseling couches are loaded with good people who just can't seem to keep commitments, follow through on promises, and seize important opportunities.

Do you have the following symptoms of an inability to say yes?

1. You have a difficult time making a decision when you have multiple choices.
2. You are unwilling to make a commitment.
3. You have turned down opportunities in the past, which you regret.

The Danger of Lost Opportunities

One of the most common reasons for a lack of yes these days is the hectic pace of life. With only so much time, money, and limited emotional capacity, we often fail to say yes to wonderful opportunities because we feel consumed. How can I say yes when I have so much else going on?

Consider that your life is like a computer. When you receive a signal that there is no more room remaining on your system, you must free up space if you hope to load any new software or files. You have to condense your files or delete some. Unlike computers, we rarely have the opportunity to add significant capacity, so our ability to say yes is often in direct proportion to our willingness to make room for the new commitment. When we are unwilling to edit our priorities and make room for what is more productive and effective, we miss out on golden opportunities.

The Danger of Duplicity

Even if we recognize our opportunities, they are practically worthless unless we act on them. Saying and doing are often very different responses. The inherent weakness in much research is that it relies too heavily on surveys and polls. What people say they believe in and what they do often are in conflict. In Western society, we have confused belief with application, assuming that if we mentally assent to an idea, we have acted on it. We are deceived if we think our behavior always conforms to our beliefs.

The Danger of the Procrastination Rut

One way we subtly get around the emotional dilemma of claiming to value something without acting on it is to procrastinate. This process engages the will and intent but not the body or action. It is akin to having the motor running with the car in park. No one can accuse us of not caring. It's clear we do because our intent is to "get around to it." Our yes is evident by our emotional support, but our real yes is avoided because, for all practical purposes, we have not acted on the yes. We hold the check in our hand but have not cashed it. Just a little more time, a bit more organization, a few more dollars or accomplishments and it's as good as done.

The problem with holding patterns is that they often become the ends in themselves, not merely transitions. Because procrastination works as both a conscience appeaser and an action avoider, we find it a convenient place to put any number of good intentions. Instead of denying a goal, we put it on a pile with other to-do items. Eventually the stacks become a storage system instead of a runway. The biggest problem with procrastination is that we stay in the holding pattern and never land. We may not even realize it and deceive ourselves by confusing intent with action.

The Danger of the Lost Integrity

The word *hypocrite* comes to mind for people who say yes but do no. The word originates from the Greek theater and means "one who wears a mask." Being two-faced is a similar description. The word *integrity* comes from the Latin word *integer,* referring to what is whole, complete. The concepts relate well to the book of James:

> If any of you lacks wisdom, he should ask God, who gives generously to all without finding fault, and it will be given to him. But when he asks, he must believe and not doubt, because he who doubts is like a wave of the sea, blown and tossed by the wind. That man should not think he will receive anything from the Lord; he is a double-minded man, unstable in all he does.
>
> James 1:5–8

After so many unfulfilled intentions, people see us as untrustworthy, unable to follow through on our commitments. This hurts us professionally as well as personally.

Fear of Saying Yes

Why do we fear to commit ourselves to worthy endeavors if our fear is self-defeating? Here are four reasons:

1. *We fear failure.* Our sense of failure can arise from several outcomes. We may find that we were wrong about our decision. We may feel rejected or misunderstood by those around us. Our commitment may have created conflict in other areas, because we stole time from relationships, borrowed money from savings, or drained energy from other priorities.

   When we have once experienced failure, we are often reluctant to commit ourselves again. We think:

What will others think or say if my decision doesn't pan out? What if people take advantage of me? I've made poor choices in the past and now I'm paranoid about repeating them. Fear creates a negative condition out of which we have to make decisions. While we need to listen to healthy fears and apprehensions that are designed to preserve us, fearful living inhibits good decision-making. I want to be careful not to overstate this idea, because, if we always go against our fears, as some imply we should, we'll develop other kinds of regrets. Keeping fear in check and doing some homework before making commitments are the wise choices.

2. *We exaggerate the costs and underestimate the benefits.* The best things in life are usually free but cost dearly. To invest in a marriage, friendship, or career often requires huge amounts of energy and dedication, but the potential payoff is priceless. When people grow and come to the next level of commitment, they often do not want to push through the barrier and do what it takes to progress, so they back off. Most worthwhile endeavors require increasing levels of commitment. For example, a start-up company may succeed but to go to the next level, there must be a large infusion of money, significant restructuring, and personnel transitions. If the business owners are unwilling to make these efforts, the business will not progress. This is not to suggest that bigger is better or that we should always commit more and more. Meaningful living requires us to say yes at times. If, at these times, we avoid the yes, we never get to experience what the yes affords.

3. *We don't know what deserves our commitment.* No one wants to waste time, energy, and ego by making the wrong decisions, so a part of making right decisions is putting in the effort to find the facts. Inves-

tigating work conditions, getting to know a person well, and doing some background work are all a part of do-diligence. When we have boned up on a subject behind a decision, it improves our odds of making the right one. When we fly by the seat of our pants, too lazy to check our references or investigate, we rightly fear wrong decisions. But when we are indecisive we may lose what we could have gained.

When we are planning to make a large purchase, comparison shopping, reading *Consumer Reports,* and talking to previous buyers help us make the best purchase decision. For other big decisions, prayer and fasting, research, and doing what is required to be well-informed are parts of making the right choice. Since our lives are pretty much the result of the decisions we have made, we can see why proper preparation is so important.

4. *We've not seen commitment modeled.* Living in a disposable society means that many of us have never learned the art of persevering and the power of commitment. We have learned from the significant others in our past and present to toss out diapers, eating utensils, clothing, copy machines, computers, and countless other items as we strive to keep up the pace. The garbage man comes by weekly, making more space for this week's throwaways. Unfortunately this attitude overlaps into churches, jobs, neighborhoods, friendships, and marriages. If they're not working, don't worry about calling a repair person, toss them; go get new ones. We grow up watching our influencers float from job to job and friend to friend. When we see our parents separate or divorce because they can't work through difficult matters, we assume by default that this is what people do.

Regardless of these background reasons, the foreground responsibility is on us. We hold the yes lever in our hands. To throw it, we run the risk of failure. Not to throw it often *guarantees* failure. Our choice makes a huge difference in our lives, if in nothing else. When people refuse to take risks, pursue new ventures, or follow through on commitments, they miss what they could have gained. The regret among the commitment-weak is grave. They celebrate birthday after birthday, with little to show for the time they've spent on earth.

Becoming Your Own Best Ally

Recognize the Timing

Lost opportunities are a matter of when as well as what. I remember finding an incredible deal on a piece of furniture that we'd wanted for some time. I wanted to make sure it was the best deal so I went to another store to price compare. When I came back to the original store, the furniture had been sold. Like the opening/closing door at the foot of the miniature golf windmill, opportunities are not usually available forever. If we do not say yes at the right time, we may not be able to say yes at all. Consider time constraints on the matter at hand. Don't assume too much or too little.

Say Yes to the Right Things

You can see the importance of prioritization and value systems when it comes to saying yes. First, you must measure against your values the opportunities that come to you. This involves the investigation we talked about earlier. If your values are poorly defined, you are wearing blinders and will be unable to make an accurate measurement. If you are not able to see the potential value among multiple opportunities, you will fail to pursue the best choice. After you have measured the opportunities against your value system, you should be able to decide which choices are the right ones, the ones that should receive top priority. As in an emergency room, you must perform triage on the array of opportunities that come your way daily. The goal is not to say yes more but to say yes to the right things for the right reasons.

Move Forward

After a military water landing, a leader ordered the delivery ships to be burned. When the soldiers turned around and saw their only means of retreat destroyed, they were motivated to fight their hardest against enormous odds. A part of making yes commitments involves removing or reducing access to the path of retreat, which is usually the course of least resistance.

It's a bad sign when people talk about changing locations for a new position and justify their yes by saying, "If things don't work out, we can always come back." God has designed us to go forward, not backward. Rarely will you give a job, relationship, or commitment a fair go of it when you keep your eyes on the exit sign. Contingency strategies are not the same as retreat plans, however. Sometimes the difference is a matter of motivation and emotion.

Plan on Persevering

This leads us to the reality check of nearly every significant *yes* we make. Worthwhile endeavors will at times be difficult and strain our innermost resources. Quitting, starting over, and running are tempting forms of retreat. Our friends Ray and Anne Ortlund explain it this way. There are three zones in nearly any life endeavor: A, B, and C.

The A Zone is where the dream is hatched. The salesman motivates us to buy. We see the possibilities. Our excitement carries us forward toward the commitment. The B Zone is the tumultuous place where reality hits, we feel like giving in, and we talk ourselves into calling it quits. The B Zone often leads to the Q (Quit) Zone. The more often we enter the Q Zone, the easier it is the next time. You can see people who repeat this cycle over and over. For those who persevere, there is a C Zone, the place where you enjoy your hard work, investment, and benefits. If you do not persevere through the B Zone, you'll never get to the C Zone where the reward of satisfaction comes.

SELF-SABOTAGE ASSESSMENT

Place a value of 1 to 5 in the box beside each statement: 1 = no/rarely 2 = infrequently 3 = sometimes 4 = usually 5 = yes/always

- [ ] 1. I like the process of making commitments.
- [ ] 2. I enjoy considering new opportunities.
- [ ] 3. I cut out existing engagements to make room for new ones.
- [ ] 4. I work on projects until they are finished.
- [ ] 5. People view me as a person who walks my talk.

Add the numbers and divide by 5. If your score is 1–2.5, you are probably being an enemy to yourself in this area. If your score is 2.6–3.75, you may want to consider this area more to see what is fuzzy or what you could do to improve it. If your score is over 3.75, you are either strong in this area or partially blind, which may require a perspective of someone who knows you well.

Self-sabotage assessment: _____

Another person's assessment of me: _____

UNPACKING PROCEDURES

1. What is one yes you made and committed to that paid off richly?
2. What is one yes you failed to make or persevere through that you now regret?
3. What was the main point you gleaned from this chapter?
4. How have you seen this behavitude played out constructively or destructively in the lives of others?
5. What are some challenges in discovering what you should and should not say yes about?
6. How can you say yes to something new in a jam-packed schedule?

three

SHOW-AND-TELL

"I don't know what went wrong. Ever since high school, I knew I wanted to make a lot of money, to leave my mark. I was sick and tired of growing up in a poor, factory worker's home. I vowed that I would not work all my life and have nothing to show for it. So I left home right after high school, slaved my way through college, went to work for a large company, climbed the ladder, used my stock benefits to start my own company, and I made money.

"I wasn't my father. Each house I bought was bigger and nicer. I did the luxury car thing, the fancy vacations, and local hobnobbing. I had my ups and downs too. My first wife left me; said I was never home and when I did show up, I was a pain to live with. She was probably right. Then I did the old singles routine, hitting the popular watering holes and flashing the cash with the babes. At the time, I thought I was on top of the world.

"As I look back, I realize how shallow I was and how shallow the people were I was trying to impress. I never had a crash-and-burn story, you know, a major heart attack at forty or bankruptcy or anything. From the outside, I've still got it all. But one morning I woke up and it was as if I got outside of myself and asked the question, *What are you doing? What contribution are you making? Why are you wasting your life pursuing more and bigger things?* I felt so embarrassed. I felt like a kid who threw a tantrum until his parents bought him this toy that he just had to have, and then he grew up and realized it was a junky piece of cheap plastic. How silly I must appear!"

Description and Dangers

The Mercedes S500 convertible license plate read: I
M DONE. Chances are, the vanity tag reflected a hope,
not reality. While you can certainly be wealthy and not
wrapped up in your possessions, just as you can be broke
and incredibly materialistic, money and materialism have
the uncanny side effect of causing you to want more. It's
like the joke about Chinese food—it tastes good, but an
hour later you're hungry again. The chic furniture store's
billboard displayed a single chair. The caption read: "How
to have a happy marriage. Buy two." That sums up the
philosophy of the self-defeating behavitude known as
materialism.

The challenge for most of us who live in a capitalistic
culture is that a significant part of our economic system is
based on the idea that the flow of money is essential to
existence. The problem is that once we have our necessi-
ties covered, the flow dwindles to a trickle because we stop
spending. Our needs are fulfilled. Then we develop the
idea that what we have now is insufficient.

Four words lead the charge: *more, newer, bigger, better.* We
need one more thing or, better yet, two. The thing we have
is out of date and, well, what would the neighbors think?
We don't want them to talk behind our back, do we? "Poor
Julie, she's worn that same dress for so long. Poor Jack,
the car he drives looks so antiquish." And if more or newer
isn't our desire, then bigger must be: bigger house, car,
boat, or diamond. And for the person who has everything,
there's always better. Why not upgrade to the luxury vehicle, more impressive address, and fancier clothes? More,
newer, bigger, and better—and easy credit—are the primary reasons behind soaring personal debt. When our
wants meet easy credit, it's like gasoline and fire.

When I was in elementary school, we had a daily time
of show-and-tell, when kids brought things from home to

show the class or told stories of things they saw or did. The competitive nature among some of us resulted in considerable bragging and even some fabricated stories. Often adults are like little kids at show-and-tell. We think the one with the most to show off is the best, smartest, coolest, most powerful, and happiest. The truth, however, may be just the opposite.

Do you have the following symptoms of being materialistic?

1. Your wish list is long, and you're under the impression that one more thing will make you happier.
2. You've leveraged yourself financially so that you have little breathing room should you have a financial setback.
3. You argue about money in your family, and you feel stressed and overworked, trying to keep up.

The Danger of Confusing Materialism with Wealth

Popular thought tells us that materialism is the same as wealth. But the two are different in nature. The first assumes that things bring happiness and satisfaction. Money and possessions, therefore, are keys to that formula.

Wealth, however, does not carry with it the idea that money makes one happy. We draw incorrect conclusions when we assume that wealthy people, or those who have nice things, are materialistic. Some of the poorest people in our society are among the most materialistic, because they are banking their satisfaction and enjoyment on money and possessions. Conversely, some of the least materialistic people I know have lots of money. They understand that wealth has its own set of hassles and does not bring the best things in life. Some of them have become wealthy because they've not squandered their money on things, and God seems to have blessed their frugality. But whether we have lots of money or little, we'll defeat ourselves by pursuing things in search of status and a sense of value in life.

The Danger of Buying the Lie

Most television is a Trojan horse. It's not what it first appears—a source of entertainment. It entertains but its real purpose is to bring commercialism into our homes. The marketing messages are successful when they produce in the viewer a sense of dissatisfaction. "You'd be happier with whatever we can provide. Poor soul, how have you made it this long without us?"

The psycho-spiritual dilemma of materialism is that we think we're getting more than we really are. Marketing gurus attach intangible benefits to their tangible products. We are told that if we use a certain shaving cream, we'll get sex appeal. The same is true of the right beer, car, blue jeans, cologne, and any number of other products, which in themselves have little or nothing to do with sexual attraction, love, intimacy, or relationships in general. Because marketers know our felt needs are basic human desires, they make big leaps in tying their products to the satisfaction of these appetites.

The Danger of Expecting Satisfaction from Things

Jesus said, "Take care! Be on your guard against all kinds of greed; for one's life does not consist in the abundance of possessions" (Luke 12:15 NRSV). When we try to satisfy spiritual and emotional cravings with things that cannot provide long-term satisfaction, we are setting ourselves up for disappointment. Marketing gurus focus on our spiritual and emotional appetites, because they know we will buy their products and services, as we try to quench our inner cravings. Unfortunately the emotional disappointment is often followed by further guilt and discouragement because of what the purchase costs us in money, time, energy, and pride.

The Danger of Miscalculating the Worth of Others

Another reason why show-and-tell is a self-defeating behavitude is that when we buy into the philosophy ourselves, we tend to perceive the value of others according to what they possess. Thus we focus on a person's possessions or position and fail to get to know him or her as an individual. This creates prejudice, alienation, and shallow acceptance. We flatter those who appear to be successful and have many possessions, and our friendships are based on appearances and bank accounts, rather than true love and acceptance. We do an injustice to ourselves when we base our friendships on economics and status. We overlook those who are wealthy but who are not materialistic, and we alienate some wonderful people who do not possess significant resources. Most of us would not be impressed with people who develop relationships with us only because of our perceived wealth, yet we do it to others. We compromise our character when we value people according to their net worth instead of their real worth.

Self-Defeating Behavior

Why do we buy into the lies of "show-and-tell"? Here are four reasons:

1. *We confuse applause with self-esteem.* Self-esteem is an awareness of our intrinsic, God-given value. When we do not have a firm grasp of the basis for our value, we easily fall into the trap of thinking we gain our

value from what others say and think about us. In a society that associates net worth with self-worth, we are motivated to achieve all we can to win the applause of others. Materialism becomes not an end in itself but a means of receiving applause.

As I said previously, the person who requires the approval and affirmation of others to establish personal worth is setting him- or herself up for a rollercoaster ride. He or she becomes susceptible to the next fad and latest marketing campaign. When a significant other suggests an investment or a label of clothing, the person buys.

Living in the Southwest, we enjoy good Mexican food. Nancy and I love to hear the sizzle of the fajitas skillet as the waiter walks toward our table. Sometimes we discover that the sizzle sounds better than the fajitas actually taste. We get sold on the sight and sound versus the substance. The applause we get for our flashy clothes, glittering chrome, sparkling jewelry, and brand-name labels is more sizzle than significance.

2. *We replace inner contents with outer contents.* At one time we had a hole in our garage wall that allowed winter wind and insects into our house. Because I'm such a lousy fix-it guy, I took the shortcut. Instead of breaking out the tools and mending it properly, I stuffed a rag into the hole.

Our lives can be like that wall. They can have emotional cavities of discontent. Eventually we will either fill the holes properly or patch them with rags. There is an obvious difference between plugging a hole and fixing it, but when we are discontent, we often try a quick fix and plug emotional holes with possessions and the activities that money can buy. We resort to what can be seen, felt, held, and owned. We lean toward tangible objects when we want to enhance our sense of security, looking for what will look best in our closet, garage, or family room. When others look at us, they don't see the holes. They say, "Hey, nice rags." These possessions don't plug the holes for long, however, because our real needs have to do with acceptance, love, and contentment, and these require time and effort to develop. Outer contents do not create inner contentment.

3. *We confuse who we are with what we do.* Often our identity is wrapped up in our work, career, and accomplishments. Because so much of our identity and worth is associated with what we do, we work hard at excelling and achieving a higher status. Usually the by-product of this climb is money, power, perks, and prestige, and we feel good about ourselves because of what we have achieved and possess.

4. *Society rewards us for what it gets from us rather than for who we are to God.* Most of our society rewards us for what we do for it. We are not valued for who we are as individuals, created in the image of God. Rather, we are affirmed by what we produce. In a way it makes sense. Human conditioning principles teach us that if we want a certain behavior, we should reward it. Good or bad, we tend to get what we reward. And this is what society does. Positive contributions are usually rewarded. Undesirable behavior, such as laziness, thievery, and other antisocial behavior, isn't. Because corporations, teams, and sometimes even families reward achievement and accomplishment with monetary and tangible goods, we begin to seek these as a way of life. The reinforcement of everyday life is so strong that we buy into that value system as if it were the whole truth about our worth.

Becoming Your Own Best Ally

Determine What Matters Most

To end this self-defeating behavitude, we need to come to terms with what really matters in life, whom we'll have to answer to, and for what we'll be held accountable. If you're a fatalist or existentialist, all you have is the here and now. Since you have no hope in anything more than your present life, you may as well live it up.

Self-centered fatalism fails to appreciate the value of investing in others. Getting beyond yourself is a key to maturity and deep satisfaction. History is full of stories of people who made it big but failed to make it good. You don't have to follow in their footsteps. You can learn from their life lessons. It's a bit like stopping people who are coming from where you're headed. By asking them about road conditions, directions, and distance, you can potentially avoid wasting your travel time and fuel.

Learn That Wealth Is Not the Answer

An interesting thing about confronting this self-defeating behavitude of materialism is that within its fulfillment is its demise. In other words, the people most apt to recognize the futility of acquiring more and more things are those who have actually done it. When people lack fulfillment as well as tangible goods, they assume that their happiness is to be found in what they do not possess. Thus they begin purchasing more, bigger, newer, and nicer. After so many houses, cars, clothes, and vacations, they begin to realize that happiness is not some destination on this trail. Until you've driven down that road a bit, you keep thinking happiness is just up ahead at the next acquisition. When you get there, you think, *It must be one more exit.*

Studies show that when people are asked, "How much money would make you feel happy and comfortable?" regardless of their annual income, nearly everyone gives the same answer—"Just a little bit more." Once you've achieved a certain number of possessions, you begin to realize that one more is not going to do it. Then you become ripe for something more meaningful. If you're wise, you won't have to go very far down the road to come to this realization.

Seek Financial Wisdom

Most of us are never taught by our parents or schools how to manage our finances. If you want to learn about budgeting, investments, and fiscal management, you will have to take the initiative yourself to learn. There are many courses, seminars, college classes, books, and certified financial planners who can help you learn a lot about financial matters. Living within your means is a major key to enjoying your wealth without becoming materialistic and bound by debt and the need for more. Money has a way of creating an appetite for more that is rarely satiated.

Give Away Your Resources

Perhaps the greatest proof that money does not have you in its grip is if you are giving it away to good causes. Even in this, however, motivation is the key. Merely seeking a tax deduction doesn't count. Philanthropic activity to gain inroads into the circles of the rich and famous and to get your picture in the social section of the newspaper is materialism disguised. In soul growth, money tends to be the final frontier because it most closely represents the seat of our priorities. It is not until our priorities change and money loses its grip on us that we are able to become spiritually mature.

The Bible speaks more of money and possessions than any other single subject (in more than 2,500 verses). The reason is that they are so attached to our self-image and soul. More than any single item, money represents power and the ability to control our destiny. When you intentionally give regular sums to your local church, respected charity, and even anonymously to people in need, you help yourself remain free from, or at least less in bondage to, materialism. Ironically, the primary benefit of giving is not the help you give to others but the discipline you develop in staying free from the addictive nature of money.

SELF-SABOTAGE ASSESSMENT

Place a value of 1 to 5 in the box beside each statement: 1 = no/rarely 2 = infrequently 3 = sometimes 4 = usually 5 = yes/always

- [ ] 1. I live within my income.
- [ ] 2. I avoid investing a lot of mental energy into thinking about what I would like to have.
- [ ] 3. I am happy to see and experience what others have without feeling envious or sad when I go home.
- [ ] 4. I am happy with what I have without complaining about it.
- [ ] 5. I avoid comparing what I have with what others have.

Add the numbers and divide by 5. If your score is 1–2.5, you are probably being an enemy to yourself in this area. If your score is 2.6–3.75, you may want to consider this area more to see what is fuzzy or what

you could do to improve it. If your score is over 3.75, you are either strong in this area or partially blind, which may require a perspective of someone who knows you well.

Self-sabotage assessment: _____

Another person's assessment of me: _____

UNPACKING PROCEDURES

1. How much income or net worth would it take to make you happy?
2. Describe someone you know who does not have much but seems appear materialistic. What are the signs of this?
3. Think of someone you know who has a lot of money but does not appear materialistic. What seem to be his or her priorities?
4. How can you live in such a possession-oriented culture and not buy into the value system of this culture?
5. Can you think of a time when you tried to satisfy a spiritual or emotional craving with something tangible?
6. Why is this behavitude self-defeating and why is it so deceptive (it often goes unnoticed by those who have it)?

four

PUPPET PEOPLE

"Beth, why did you hit your children?"
"They were misbehaving. I tried talking to them and that didn't seem to work. Then I yelled and screamed, and that didn't help. I just lost it."
"So you felt like you had no other options?"
"No, they were driving me nuts and I had to do something."
"I agree. You did need to do something. But I'm wondering why you chose what you did."
"It wasn't a choice. Don't you see? They're the ones that were kicking and screaming. They made me angry. They *made* me hit them."

Description and Dangers

I worked my way through college, partly as a professional ventriloquist. Kids were fascinated and adults amused. Often people would ask, "How do you do it? How do you work your dummy? He seems so lifelike." Every above-average ventriloquist knows how easy it is to direct attention from yourself to the vent figure (dummy), just by pulling a few levers. But people are not dummies. They were not created to be controlled by others.

Puppet people are those who allow others to pull their strings and then blame those others for their helplessness. When we let others pull our strings, we inevitably wind up with regrets, diminished self-esteem, and feelings of powerlessness.

Do you have the following symptoms of being a puppet person?

1. You commonly blame failures, decisions, and your emotional responses on other people.
2. You resent being manipulated by people who try to influence you.
3. You procrastinate and then make decisions without input from others. When you decide, you worry about how the others will respond.

The Danger of Not Exercising Your Free Will

When we let others determine our responses, we tend to overlook an incredible, God-given feature in human nature—our free will. When we ignore our free will, we sacrifice numerous opportunities to step out on faith, stand up for what is right, and take life by the horns, so to speak. The person who has relinquished the power to choose must either be satisfied with the leftovers or find someone on whose coattails he or she can ride into glory. The world is full of people who blame circumstances, other people, bad luck, and God for their demise. They naively wander through life, proving to themselves they are victims of circumstance, when all the while they had within reach the solution to many of their self-induced problems.

The Danger of Denying Our Value System

Bowing to peer pressure is little more than giving up our willpower and following the will of others. Throughout life, we are put to the test in terms of values, character, and priorities. No matter how well-intentioned we are to uphold our values, we will consistently compromise them if we lack the ability to cut the strings that others are trying to pull. And pull them they will. "Do not conform any longer to the pattern of this world, but be transformed by the renewing of your mind. Then you will be able to test and approve what God's will is—his good, pleasing and perfect will" (Rom. 12:2). We have little chance of doing God's will or our own if we conform to the influence of others. The guilt, humiliation, and inner anger that follow value compromise can be unbearable. As a result of string-pulling, we either lower our standards or run away from them the rest of our lives.

The Danger of Diminished Self-Respect

The burden of free will is evident from the very beginning of humanity. We'd much rather blame our emotions and decisions on circumstances and people than bear responsibility for misbehaving. When God confronted the first couple, the man blamed the woman for giving him the forbidden fruit. On top of that, he qualified the woman, "You know, the one that *you* (God) gave me," extending the blame warranty to God. The woman in turn passed the buck to the serpent for her disobedience. Of course, everyone knows who created the serpent in the first place. The problem with the blame game is that we eventually mar our self-esteem in the process, pretending to be helpless victims as opposed to willing conspirators.

The Danger of Making Wrong Decisions

The older I get, the more people I meet who have major regrets in life, often traceable to the ill-effects of letting someone pull their strings. Every week in any city, you can read about the regrets of people who let others talk them into doing something against their better judgment. We become pawns of evil forces when we cannot effectively pull our own strings. When we live out the will of others, we end up regretting our decision.

I have a friend who has helped a relative of his build a very powerful business. All the while, he assumed a support role and has not been remunerated in kind as the business has grown. He told me, "I let him use me. I don't stick up for myself. I do whatever he asks. And I resent the way I've helped make him rich, while I'm working my head off for his company."

Relinquishing Control

Why do we let people pull our strings when it is self-defeating? Here are four reasons:

1. *We're unwilling to take responsibility for our own actions.* Living with the ramifications of our responses and accepting the results of our decisions can be hefty undertakings. Like an overweight backpack or bag of groceries, the burden can make even the strongest of us at times yearn for relief. When the decisions have resulted in less than optimal outcomes, carrying that weight becomes drudgery. Most boomers remember Flip Wilson's one-liner, "The devil made me do it." And many of us would like to claim that excuse for our choices, but while circumstances may seem to dictate our feelings and, in turn, our decision-making, nearly all of the time we have the power to choose our responses. Faulting kids, spouses, bosses, employees, and associates for the way we feel and act is relinquishing what is perhaps our most Godlike quality—free will.

2. *We rent versus own our core values.* When we have not predetermined our basic value system, we are vulnerable to the influence of those around us. It's like renting our values. When you rent a home, you are far less apt to fix it up than when you own it, and renters are more likely to move than owners. Ownership instills pride, identity, and motivation. In a similar way, renting our values makes us less likely to stand up against others' opinions and intimidation tactics, allowing them to pull our strings. Peer pressure is not just an adolescent issue. It is a very real motivator for the adult as well. Relying on others for our priorities, values, and ultimately our attitudes and behaviors creates a condition that puts others in the driver's seat of our lives. Then, because we are not settled in our beliefs, we are susceptible to all sorts of regrettable events. Determining our nonnegotiables in advance allows us to stick with them when people and circumstances encourage us to do otherwise.

3. *We overestimate what we'll get from complying.* The allure of nearly all temptations is the payoff. Gangs convince would-be members that membership has huge privileges. The wits'-end parent feels that screaming at the kids will bring the desired peace, without considering the cost in security and self-esteem of the children. Girlfriends think that taking off their clothes for their boyfriends will foster the intimacy and commitment that they seek. Wives let husbands intimidate them, hoping their compliance will iron out the wrinkles in the marriage. These are but a few of the countless examples of everyday attitudes and actions that show we overestimate the benefits and underestimate the costs and potential damage of letting others pull our strings.

4. *Too much of our identity is based on social relationships.* Self-image is key when it comes to bucking the influence of others and taking responsibility for our own behavitudes. When we base our sense of value on how others respond to us, we become vulnerable to people tides. Like a boat without a mooring, we go back and forth, up and down, depending on the nearest and strongest current of the moment.

Chameleons take on the color of their surroundings. Low–self-esteem people meld with the present environment. To fit in, they compromise their values so as to win acceptance from others. The problem intensifies when two contradictory forces act on them at the same time. Like high and low pressure weather systems colliding, the storm clouds loom large. Inner turmoil is quite common in the person who is easily influenced by others. The first phase of the turmoil is created by the conflicting values. The second phase of turmoil is created by the guilt and grief of compromise and the consequences of bad decisions.

Becoming Your Own Best Ally

Transform Your Mind

"Do not conform any longer to the pattern of this world, but be transformed by the renewing of your mind." Another way of looking at Romans 12:1 is: Don't let other people pull your strings. The temptation to copycat, do as they do, conform, and comply will always be in front of you. You're swimming against the current most days of the week. But this need not intimidate you. The goal is to be transformed by renewing your mind, changing the way you look at life, others, yourself, and your objectives. Only you can live your life. Other people may want you to live according to their wishes. True friends, people who love you, will not try to pull your strings.

Understand String-Pullers

Why do people pull others' strings? Understanding the puppeteer mind-set is not necessarily vital for us to resist it, but it can help. The person trying to control you may be a master puppeteer. Some of the most effective at it are subtle, not appearing manipulative or overt, and their motivations are manifold. The spiritual answer to our question is sin. The essence of sin is trying to be in control, be your own god. This easily spills over into trying to control other people as well. Self-centered people try to get us to conform to their ways for their own personal benefit. This is manipulation. Healthy persuasion is when you try to influence another person to change his or her ways for his or her benefit, not yours. The reason for string-pulling may revolve around early-life modeling, a controlling parent or the inverse, an overly lax or absent parent. Either situation may produce a string-puller.

When you identify a puppeteer or string-puller, work hard not to overcompensate. Sometimes we let people think they are making our decisions and then we do the opposite of what they want, regardless of what is best for us. For example, you're in a furniture store, shopping for a couch. You see it. The salesman sees you see it. He swoops down for the kill. Even though you really like the sofa, you dislike the pressure you're now feeling to sign the papers and accept delivery before the end of the week. You recognize string-pulling behavior, which you resent. Irritated by the pressure and not wanting to give in to a puppeteer, you walk out of the store, leaving your desired couch on the showroom floor. While the string-puller did not win, neither did you. You let the salesman's behavior determine your decision. An alternative would have been to ask for another salesperson, request that he leave you alone for a while, or write down the details about the couch and then phone in your order. This way you would make the decision that is best for you without letting a puppeteer inordinately influence you positively or negatively.

Grow Up!

Most people tend to confuse chronological age with maturity. We assume that as we experience more and more birthdays, we get smarter, better, and more complete. Unfortunately there is no direct correlation between time and maturation, only the potential for it.

When we become adults emotionally, we put childish ways behind us. The big difference between adults and children is responsibility. We don't put kids in roles or positions that require responsibility because they are immature and unable to handle it. When we become mature adults, we take responsibility for our actions.

Accepting responsibility begins by realizing we have the right to choose our responses. Shouldering responsibility often becomes a stressful and tedious thing. When we're tired or depleted, we are prone to unload this burden. In doing so we become vulnerable to the string-pulling of others. Within most people is a desire to control that tempts them to pull strings and manipulate others when given the chance. This dynamic, push-pull battle for control rarely subsides in normal, everyday social interactions. The potential for having our strings pulled is constant. Those who lack the inner fortitude to combat this pressure forfeit their destinies to the whims of those who use them but do not love them. Mature people love the best. The biblical definition of *love* is that it is a choice, a decision to treat another person with honor and as one who is valuable, created in the image of God. This love is not based on emotions, hormones, what you do for me, or how you respond to me. This love does not blame others for unloving attitudes and actions. People who love us maturely do not pull our strings. And if we love them maturely we don't try to pull theirs.

Recognize Weak Moments

Perhaps the most common string-pulling condition is when we choose to respond with anger instead of healthy, loving communication. Letting people pull our chains and push our buttons is most common when we are emotionally vulnerable. Overreacting often results in doing or saying things we regret later.

During a seminar, a counselor taught a simple acronym that has been helpful to me. I don't know the source of the principles, but here it is for your use: HALT—underreact when you're Hungry, Angry, Late, Tired. Knowing when we're more vulnerable to string-pulling and button-pushing empowers us to intentionally underreact and hopefully allow us to take responsibility for our attitudes and actions.

In every situation we can choose to react or respond. Reacting denotes string-pulling. Responding indicates that we accept responsibility for our behavior. I remember as a child, growing up on a farm in Iowa, my father taught me to drive the tractor when I was about ten. He sat behind me in the same seat and let me steer. When I began to swerve too far to the left or right, he would place his hand on the wheel and realign us. When we came to a narrow or rutty area, I would let him steer by himself, taking my hands off the wheel.

When we let other people get their hands on our steering wheel, we relinquish our God-given ability to exercise free will. This often results in self-defeat. Keep your hands on the wheel. Seek God and others for help, but know that the power to choose is always in you.

SELF-SABOTAGE ASSESSMENT

Place a value of 1 to 5 in the box beside each statement: 1 = no/rarely 2 = infrequently 3 = sometimes 4 = usually 5 = yes/always

☐ 1. I am aware when other people are trying to pull my strings.

☐ 2. I am able to take responsibility for my actions and responses and do not blame others.

☐ 3. I commonly resist others' influence when it goes against what I believe is best.

☐ 4. I consistently enjoy the decisions and responses I make.

☐ 5. I recognize puppeteering behaviors in others.

Add the numbers and divide by 5. If your score is 1–2.5, you are probably being an enemy to yourself in this area. If your score is 2.6–3.75, you may want to consider this area more to see what is fuzzy or what you could do to improve it. If your score is over 3.75, you are either strong in this area or partially blind, which may require a perspective of someone who knows you well.

Self-sabotage assessment: _____

Another person's assessment of me: _____

UNPACKING PROCEDURES

1. What is a common string-pulling behavior you've seen?
2. Who is a puppeteer in your life or circle of influence?
3. Describe a time when you let someone else pull your strings.
4. Describe a time when you intentionally resisted another's string-pulling.
5. How do you try to pull others' strings?
6. What do you think about the concept that most people are not emotionally mature in the way they love?
7. Can you think of anyone who seems to be a good model of mature love? Why do you think this?

five

HE'LL/SHE'LL
MAKE ME HAPPY

"What's the matter with you?" Janet asked. "When we were dating, you always wanted to go out, have fun, be with friends. Now all you want to do is sit around and watch the boob tube."

"I do not," Jeff retorted. "Look who's talking. You used to be a slim 125 pounds. Now you've ballooned up to who knows what. It takes two to have fun."

"Hey, I'm ready. I've been asking you to go out every night this week, but you'd rather channel surf and check your e-mail than spend any quality time together."

"Right. Well, maybe you're not so fun to be around anymore. Have you ever thought of that?"

"Jeff, you've become a hermit, a modern caveman. You work, come home, watch TV or the computer screen, go to bed, and do it all over again. This is not what I bargained for. What about me? What am I supposed to do with my life?" Janet pleaded.

"If you don't want to be in this relationship, no one is forcing you. I am who I am. Take it or leave it."

"Don't tempt me," she said. "I'll call your bluff, and then you'll be sorry."

Description and Dangers

One of the most common, debilitating dilemmas is depending on others for our happiness. The bottom line is that if we're not happy by ourselves, we won't be happy with someone else. How many times have I heard single people tell me how much they wished they could find the right person so they could be satisfied? Sometimes in the same day, I'll counsel married people who claim they'd be happy if only they could be single again. The problem in both cases is the same, self-destructive root—depending on others to make them happy. People set themselves up for disappointment and frustration when they expect others to meet their needs and give them satisfaction.

The apostle Paul said, "I have learned to be content whatever the circumstances" (Phil. 4:11). Contentment is found in spiritual power and connection with God, not in material goods or even in relationships. When we expect our spouse, boss, employees, work associates, children, friends, pastor, or even strangers to meet all our needs, we are setting ourselves up to be disappointed.

Do you have the following symptoms of trying to find fulfillment in other people?

1. You keep looking for that one person who will make you happy.
2. You keep being disappointed, because as you get to know people, they let you down and/or you discover weaknesses.
3. You blame your unhappiness on others, as if they exist to bring you satisfaction.

The Danger of False Assumptions

How presumptuous we are when we think that others exist to make us happy! The professor taught us in Philosophy 101 that when you begin with a wrong assumption, you'll get a wrong conclusion, even if it is logical. When you have a hard day at work, you come home, expecting some hugs and empathetic talk. What you get is a husband who is stressed out over his job and has neither the patience nor capacity to respond as you desire. Because of his less-than-positive reaction, you give him the cold shoulder and turn your back to him in bed. The negative cycle begins, so that by the end of the week, you're both irritated and alienated. This is the dominant marital practice in many if not most homes. We end up perceiving the people we love most as enemies. *After all,* she thinks, *if he really loved me, he'd meet my needs.* Because most of our love is conditional in its natural state, we do not love those who are unloving toward us.

The Danger of Using People

Some people use others as if they were using a computer or a hammer. The "user" is actually a materialist, not a humanist. This person transforms everyone he can into some sort of prostitute, a body for pleasure, void of personality or great worth. The boss with this thinking treats people according to their talents or abilities and little more. When they're burned out, the boss disposes of them to find fresher talent whose life force the company can drain. The employee with this attitude uses companies to climb the ladder for his or her benefit and only associates with people who can help him or her step up one more rung. The womanizer seeks new flesh for sport. The "manizer" has arisen in our liberated society of equals and seeks men for her entertainment.

One reason our society is so mobile, uncommitted, and quick to jump from relationship to relationship is that so many have bought the idea that happiness or fulfillment is found in people. When we don't find it in sufficient quantities in one person, we look for it in someone else, much like a prospector jumping from stream to stream to find gold.

The Danger of Isolation

When, through difficult experiences, people discover that others were not created to make them happy, they sometimes choose to become emotional hermits. They pretend that they don't need other people. "I'm self-sufficient; go away." Their emotional isolation incarcerates them in prisons of loneliness and even depression. By losing touch with others they become vulnerable to blind spots, making mistakes, and alienating people whom they keep at a distance. Nearly always this behavitude is a defensive response by someone who has been hurt and is either in denial or intentionally guarded to prevent future pain.

The Danger of Limited Life Enjoyment

On our farm we had a water tank in the barnyard that provided water to our house. To the best of my memory, it was about fifteen feet tall and perhaps eight feet in diameter. I remember my dad tapping the side of the wooden receptacle, estimating the water level. When it was low, he would send me down the lane to turn on the windmill. The metal blades whirled in the breeze, generating a pump that drew water from a well beside a stream. If you didn't understand the system and wondered where we got our water, you might think the source was the wooden water tank, but the tank would eventually go dry. Ultimately the water source was the well below the windmill.

People are like that wooden tank. They can dispense much joy to us, but any one person will never provide sufficient resources to make us happy. If we depend on people for our happiness, over time we will lose hope and become disappointed.

When we are taught early in life that we need to get along with people, pick good friends, and avoid negative kids, we may begin to assume that people are needed to make us happy. Experiencing joy through certain people may cause us to assume that is why they exist. Materialists believe that things make you happy; obtain all you can. Humanists trust the idea that people make you happy; find the right ones. But spiritual people recognize that happiness lies outside of things and people. The apostle Paul writes, "And my God will meet all your needs according to his glorious riches in Christ Jesus" (Phil. 4:19). When God becomes the source of our fulfillment, satisfaction, and even happiness, it takes the pressure off our other relationships.

Growing up in the Midwest, I learned to be cautious about walking on a frozen pond in the winter because the ice might crack and I'd fall into the freezing water. Solid-seeming ice might be weak and could break under pressure.

On the lake of life, God is solid. He can handle the pressures we place on him. When we put too much weight on our relationships, expecting people to meet our needs and make us happy, the relationship often cracks and we fall through. But God invites us to trust him and put our faith in his power and provision. God has infinite ways to meet our needs and give us peace. He may use songs, books, friends, strangers, ideas, nature, and many other things to bring us fulfillment. Don't limit his provision to a few loved ones and associates. When you sense a need, pray, turn it over to him, and let him meet it in the way he knows is best.

Expecting People to Make Us Happy

Why do we focus on other people as the source of our fulfillment? Here are four reasons:

1. *We confuse the desire for affirmation with the need for affirmation.* As the Iron Curtain was falling and just after the revolution in Romania, I made a trip there to the northern region. By that time the world had heard about the Romanian orphanages, where scores of abandoned children were kept alive in mass facilities. There was no time for cuddling, holding, or touching. Feeding and changing diapers was the maximum of care that could be expected, not the minimum. The result was that many of these kids never developed as they should, because physical touch and love are vital to children. Studies prove this.

   But external love is not an adult need. We want and enjoy it as adults, but when it becomes a need, we resort to childish living. One significant step toward maturing is being able to discern between a want and a need. Unfortunately we become our own enemies when we confuse the yearning of a desire with a need.

2. *We're stuck in child-oriented imprinting.* Internal love is a human need to recognize our God-given value. This comes by understanding God's unconditional love for us, by fostering a healthy self-image, and by receiving love as children. When, as adults, we require outside love to feel good about ourselves, we place demands on people they cannot or may choose not to fulfill. Often adults who did not receive love as children are challenged in their self-esteem. The external love they receive can serve as a tool to assure their inner value, but when it is required, it is a sign

of immaturity. Because humans are born with a capacity for, but not a developed sense of, inner love, we must learn either consciously, subconsciously, or both that we are valuable for who we are, not for what we do. If immature, we become emotionally dependent on others for our happiness.

The big job of parenting is to help kids grow through each stage of development, resulting in fully functioning adults. When we have not become functioning adults, we are often "stuck" at pre-adult stages where we continue to depend on others to meet our needs. Even though we are employed, bill-paying, educated people, we continue to dwell in the emotional nursery. Sometimes professional counseling is required to help us progress. For many, becoming aware of this tendency is sufficient to help them develop into independent adults.

3. *People often blame others for their lack of happiness.* Listen to practically any group of people for a length of time and you are apt to hear them blaming their woes in life on the actions or inactions of others. When we become aware of this behavitude, we are amazed at the number of pity parties we throw for ourselves, elevating the power that other people have over us. You'd think the entire world exists to make us happy. We all sing our version of the country western song, "Hey, won't ya play, another somebody-done-somebody-wrong song?" And we think that if we're all blaming our unhappiness on the random acts of unkindness of others, it must be okay.

4. *We perceive happiness as an outside versus an inside job.* Our society does a good job of teaching that happiness comes from external happenings. It's what people do for us, what they give us, how they praise us that make us happy. The truth, as we've seen, is that happiness develops within us as we

learn to trust God, reach out to others, and enjoy God's creation and the life he's given us.

One joy I have, living in Scottsdale, is that most days of the year I can count on the sun shining. I'm a sunshine person. But if I based my happiness on blue skies, I'd be in trouble on the handful of cloudy days. I would not be healthy if I based my life attitude on the weather, on what happens outside. It is the same when we allow our attitude to be determined by how other people respond to us. It is unhealthy and we undercut our potential. Happiness that is consistent and endures is an inside game. Giving up control to the random acts of kindness and meanness of others is putting our joy in their hands. This approach to life is destined to be filled with heartbreak and disappointment.

Becoming Your Own Best Ally

Set Your Own Thermostat

In one area of our staff offices, we have a thermostat on a wall in an inner room. When the door is locked, we cannot get to the thermostat to change the temperature in the outer offices. On occasion I've not had the key to unlock the door and change the temperature. Hot or cold, I've had to endure.

In its early days, our church held its worship services in rented facilities. The owners of the building kept the thermostat locked so that no one could change it. Summers in Scottsdale can be unbearably hot, while our winters can be chilly in the mornings. Our lack of control created times of irritation when the cold or heat made the rooms uncomfortable. It's interesting how much room temperature can affect our attention span and our patience.

When you believe that the thermostat controlling your happiness is outside of yourself, you will frequently be frustrated. You become your own worst enemy when you put your emotional climate control in someone else's area of responsibility and hand that person the key. Don't lock yourself out. When your comfort zone is under the control of other people and circumstances, your emotions are held hostage by what they do. When you become frustrated enough with the situation and take control, you will discover happiness. The happiest people have developed an internal locus of control, relying less on outside factors to determine their emotional state and more on themselves and their relationship with God. Whether the sky is blue or gray, bills are paid or unpaid, circumstances are positive or negative, or others are loving or unloving, such people can still be happy. That makes no sense if you buy into the external locus of control.

Ironically, because most people are externally oriented, when you are a happy person, you'll influence others to behave positively toward you. The more people respond positively to you, the easier it is to maintain a good attitude and joyful outlook.

Raise Hopes—Lower Expectations

The formula for good relationships is to have high hopes and low expectations. The tendency is the reverse. We expect a lot from people and have low hopes, because we have been let down so much in the past. We interact with others with jaded emotions, assuming that they'll fail us again. This cynical approach to life tarnishes would-be friendships. Our attitudes become self-fulfilling prophecies, and so we go from person to person, keeping our expectations beyond what others can achieve, but letting our hope drop through the floor. We don't want to be that way. We want to believe in people, but they keep letting us down.

When you change your approach and keep your hopes high and your expectations low, you remain positive and do not set people up to fail you. Lower the bar but stay upbeat. After all, people do not exist for your entertainment or pleasure.

Make God Your Main Source

The beautiful thing about seeking God as your resource center is that it takes the pressure off your relationships with people, so they can be who they are. Relationships do not respond well to demands. They develop best when given space. People intuitively sense self-serving behavior and tend to pull away from those who hang onto them dependently. When they cannot physically withdraw, as in a family or work setting, they pull back emotionally. But when you are not expecting others to make you happy, you can draw close to them without fear of being let down and they can respond to you because they won't feel used.

By focusing on God, expecting him to meet your deepest needs, you will find great fulfillment, while your relationships with people are freed from demands and expectations.

Enjoy People

The best hotels give you more than what you expect. The added pluses, such as a doorman, chocolates on your turned-down bed at night, shoes shined, and no charge for local phone calls, make you want to come back again and again. When you allow your emotional needs to be met by a caring, all-sufficient Deity, you begin to see the pluses you gain from your human relationships as pleasant extras. The kudos, laughs, hugs, and interactions with others are equivalent to complimentary desserts.

Because God's care is the entrée, you have your needs covered. You no longer expect people to make you happy. They are not your primary source of fulfillment in life. If they do not come through for you, no problem, because God is your supplier. If they do come through for you, that's just extra to be enjoyed. Gaining love, acceptance, and affirmation from others is a by-product of a life lived for God, not the main goal. When your sense of need takes precedence, you end up demanding from others what they cannot consistently provide. By expecting God alone to meet your needs, you avoid the pain of continual letdowns and disappointments.

SELF-SABOTAGE ASSESSMENT

Place a value of 1 to 5 in the box beside each statement: 1 = no/rarely 2 = infrequently 3 = sometimes 4 = usually 5 = yes/always

- ☐ 1. When others let me down a lot, I am able to move on without being upset.
- ☐ 2. I maintain a positive mood despite the moods of others.
- ☐ 3. I tend to be happy regardless of the circumstances.
- ☐ 4. I avoid pressuring people into making me happy.
- ☐ 5. I avoid blaming other people when I am upset.

Add the numbers and divide by 5. If your score is 1–2.5, you are probably being an enemy to yourself in this area. If your score is 2.6–3.75, you may want to consider this area more to see what is fuzzy or what you could do to improve it. If your score is over 3.75, you are either strong in this area or partially blind, which may require a perspective of someone who knows you well.

Self-sabotage assessment: _____

Another person's assessment of me: _____

UNPACKING PROCEDURES

1. Describe a person you know who seems to be happy regardless of his or her circumstances or relationships. How does he or she seem able to do this?
2. What frustrates you most about others? What are your relational hot buttons?
3. Think of a recent situation when someone disappointed you. How would you have responded differently had you applied the principle of raising hopes and lowering expectations in relationships?
4. What can you do to avoid seeking the attention and applause of others?
5. You don't want to become an emotional hermit, so what can you do to keep your hopes high while lowering your expectations of others?
6. What can you do to depend on God instead of other people for your need-filling?

six

INVESTING IN JUNK BONDS

Bill had major regrets. He was an ambitious go-getter in the construction business. His supervisor had put him in charge of an increasing number of projects. The extra pay and prestige made Bill feel good about what he was doing. Sure, it required him to get up early before his wife and kids were up and often took him away at dinnertime and a few weekends, but it was for his family anyway, wasn't it? Now they could buy a bigger home, wear nicer clothes, and live the good life.

But after a few years, Bill began to sense increasing tension at work with his boss and subcontractors. He began to go to the bar after work and relax a bit before coming home. He rarely got to interact with the kids except on weekends, and at times, these interactions were laced with anger and impatience. Bill's relationship with his wife was strained. Lovemaking was an infrequent event. One day his wife announced that she and the kids were leaving. She did not want to live with him and put up with the many hours of loneliness, arguing, and fear of his anger.

"What can I do to fix my family?" he pleaded with me. "I was doing it for them, so they'd have more. It's my job to provide, isn't it?"

Description and Dangers

Beer commercials are some of the most creative advertisements. One of them depicts two young men, standing at a checkout counter with groceries, supplies, and a pack of beer. They empty their pockets of all their money and come up short. Something has to go back on the shelf. One by one, the food items disappear. The only remaining supplies are the beer and the toilet paper. After a moment of desperate consideration, the TP goes back. When the checker asks the customers if they want plastic or paper, they respond in unison, "Paper!" and then grab the paper receipt out of the clerk's hand. The advertisers portrayed the priority of the men, hoping we'd have the same one.

Do you have the following symptoms of misprioritizing?

1. You work hard but find little enjoyment in life as a whole.
2. You feel out of balance, pulled into things you don't enjoy doing, with growing resentment.
3. You get into increasing debt, striving to obtain what those around you have.

The Danger of Developing Regrets

If you were down to your last five dollars and instead of baby food, milk, and staples, you bought a candy bar, pack of cigarettes, and beer, people might consider you foolish because you wasted your resources. The principle holds true for the rest of life. We are given only a limited amount of resources to invest in life, only so much time, talent, brain cells, money; we are entrusted with only a few loved ones and other relationships. When we invest these precious resources in practices that do not pay off, we develop significant regrets. When we fail to value the people who love us, we eventually reap the loss. The world is full of people who misappropriate their investments and gain remorse as a result. Running the rat race, using people, loving things, and pursuing greener grass all end up in the same place—regret.

The Danger of Letting Good Things Take the Place of the Best

In a free society where we can pretty much avoid coercive relationships that dictate our choices, we become our own worst enemies by choosing the wrong priorities. We may think that we don't waste our life, that everything we do is important. Maybe so, but the problem is often not so much that we pursue frivolous things as it is that we allow good things to take the place of the best. Instead of going home to wrestle with the kids, we put in another two to three hours of work. Instead of using our drive time to interact with our family, we make another call on our cell phone. Instead of making love with our spouse, we watch another television show or respond to our e-mail. The subtle deception is that while we're misprioritizing, alarms rarely go off, strobes don't flash, and the world pretty much lets us squander our reserves to our own demise.

The Danger of Losing Out on Best Things

The law of sowing and reaping interplays throughout our daily lives. This law of nature works in two ways. We harvest what we plant. When we plant corn, we reap corn. When we plant beans, we reap beans. When we invest in the wrong things, we're going to get the wrong results.

The second way the law of the harvest works is that we get more than what we plant. Sometimes the yield is double the amount, sometimes triple, and may even be a hundredfold. This is true of weeds as well. If we plant weeds, over time, we will get a lot more of them than we originally planted. Weeds often have beautiful blossoms, green leaves, and may look appealing. But a weed is a weed, no matter how attractive it may appear for a while, and eventually it will take over the whole garden.

We may invest in good things and get good things from life, but if we want to harvest the best, we must plant and cultivate the best.

The Danger of Blaming Others

We only worsen the situation when we come up empty-handed at the end of a year, decade, or even life and blame circumstances and people for not warning us. We assumed the little squeaks and squawks we heard were merely life adjustments, certainly not signals, warning us that we were missing something. We did not see the signs early enough and ignored our premonitions. Like so many people who wind up in counseling offices, bars, and large but lonely homes, we realize we're living "lives of quiet desperation." We may want to blame others for not pointing out to us our wrong choices, but blame is a useless activity. We are responsible for what we have done with our lives.

Choosing the Wrong Priorities

Why do we misprioritize when it is self-defeating? Here are four reasons:

1. *Ignorance.* All of our priorities are based on value systems. When we buy into a certain value system, consciously or unconsciously, we assign varying values to things such as people, friends, family, work,

material goods, exercise, spiritual growth, and so on. Change the system and you rearrange the priorities. When we are ignorant of better value systems or even unaware of the value system we're living in, we run the risk of developing significant regrets.

2. *We let the media and culture influence us.* We are significantly influenced by our surroundings. As social beings, we look to people for cues, receiving them from those on stage or screen, via writing, or in person. We cannot be totally aloof from our environment. Media influences what we believe to be valuable. I find it quite interesting how media representatives talk out of both sides of their mouth. Because ours is a free speech culture, they tell us that they are not responsible for the actions and beliefs of the people who hear or see their messages. Then they turn around and tell potential advertisers how powerful an influence they are in selling products and services. You cannot *not* communicate values. Cultures that value goods focus attention on obtaining material possessions. Cultures that elevate the value of family put a significant emphasis on family issues. When our culture elevates certain values over others, we are tempted to adopt these as well.

3. *We assume people in our sphere of influence know best.* Significant people in our lives, because of their influence and credibility, give us value cues. If someone is proficient at a certain sport, job, or role, we assume he is superior in other areas as well. That is why we see movie stars endorsing any number of products, services, or ideologies merely because of their fame, not their expertise. We're all influenced by those around us at work, church, the community, family, and friends. While receiving positive cues from these people, we can also be pressured negatively. When we look to other people for our cues, we begin to

identify what we see in these people with what is right. In democratically oriented societies, we are especially influenced to believe that the majority is correct, regardless of what our value system suggests. The majority-rules value overlooks the mistaken idea that people can be deceived en masse.

4. *We are nearsighted.* By nature, people tend to look at life from a nearsighted perspective. We base our reality system on what we experience, what is familiar. We need 20/20 spiritual vision to discern what is and is not important. When we allow good to take the place of best, it's easy to convince ourselves that we are living as we should. And then when missed opportunities and regrets pop up, we are confused. *How come I'm not experiencing more fulfillment, satisfaction, and effectiveness in life? Why do I feel I'm missing out on something?*

Becoming Your Own Best Ally

Confront the Inconsistencies

The first step in undoing the self-sabotaging behavitude of misprioritization is to confront the inconsistencies in what you say and do. If you say exercise is a top value but never get around to it, is it truly a value? When you claim family time is a priority but let school, work, and hobbies interfere, what is really important to you?

You must identify the value and priority tensions in your life. Here's how: List known discrepancies between what you view as a priority and what you spend your time doing. If you dare, ask those who know you well to make a list. Let people tell you what they hear you say and what they see you do. A more concrete approach is to list what you believe to be the top five priorities in your life and review last month's schedule and bank account (check-book or debit report) to see how much time and money you spent on these top five. Inevitably you will do your highest priorities, not what you *say* are important. Think about why there is inconsistency. What reasons or excuses do you give for not pursuing your priorities? Do you say certain things are priorities because they sound good, because social pressure requires you to mention them, or because you have been conditioned?

Value What Is Worthy

The next step toward healthy prioritizing is to make sure you value what actually has worth. Pursuing the best values is a lifelong journey for those who want to avoid self-sabotage in this area. Value hunters do what it takes to act on something of worth when they find it.

The kingdom of heaven is like treasure hidden in a field. When a man found it, he hid it again, and then in his joy went and sold all he had and bought that field.

Again, the kingdom of heaven is like a merchant look-ing for fine pearls. When he found one of great value, he went away and sold everything he had and bought it.

Matthew 13:44–46

Discovering a value may be nine-tenths of the process, but the final tenth of implementing it in your life is just as crucial.

Once you find something in life that you see has worth, you will probably do what it takes to invest in it. The prob-lem with so many of us is that we do not see the value in friendships, marriage, parenting, soul growth, and the character elements of faith, hope, and love. We buy into the world's values because we assume that the media and majority are right, simply because they are so prevalent.

God has given each of us the ability to choose what we value. When people live contrary to biblical values, they experience frustrations over the long haul. You can disagree or choose not to take the Bible seriously, but unless you've found something that works better, I recommend you seriously consider reorganizing your life around what the Bible states is worthwhile.

Order Values Appropriately

The third step is to order your values appropriately, not letting good things take the place of the best—watching that priorities 1–3 do not become 4–6 and vice versa. When we do the right thing at the wrong time it becomes . . . the wrong thing.

One day on our farm in Iowa, my dad and I were standing in a soybean field, admiring the crop. He pointed to a large, skinny stalk standing out in the field. "What's that?" he asked.

I looked at him strangely. "That's a corn stalk," I responded.

"No, it's a weed," he said.

We had hundreds of acres of corn. He knew better than that. "No, it's a corn stalk," I persisted.

"No, a stalk of corn in a soybean field is a weed."

When good things take the place of best things, and when you spend your time pursuing valuable causes when you ought to be doing other things, you are cultivating weeds.

Timing is an essential part of prioritizing. "[God] has made everything beautiful in its time" (Eccles. 3:11). Our lack of proper timing makes good things ugly. As a pastor, I'm constantly being pulled in multiple directions. I could work 24-7 and not meet the needs within our congregation. But if I am counseling or planning an event when I should be playing ball with my kids or dating my wife, I've misprioritized and life soon becomes ugly, irritating, and less than it should be.

Schedule Top Priorities

The fourth step is to daily set the agenda of your prioritization. There are things you need to accomplish daily that take precedent over other things. There are also weekly and monthly priorities. You must decide what your personal values are and resist adopting the values of others. Take responsibility so that you don't invest all of your energy into either doing other people's priorities or helping them do theirs. No one has a gun to your head. You are the primary agenda-setter in your life. There are times when you need to do your priorities without explanation. When others are involved in pursuing their priorities and your priorities collide with theirs, you have to decide how important it is for you to do your priority at that time. Communication and negotiation may be necessary. Know what is valuable and pursue those things in the appropriate time and sequence without blaming people and circumstances for your misprioritization.

___

SELF-SABOTAGE ASSESSMENT

Place a value of 1 to 5 in the box beside each statement: 1 = no/rarely 2 = infrequently 3 = sometimes 4 = usually 5 = yes/always

☐ 1. I am finding overall fulfillment in my relationships.

☐ 2. I am finding overall fulfillment in my work and leisure time.

☐ 3. I find it relatively easy to establish time priorities.

☐ 4. People who know me feel confident about my priorities.

☐ 5. I do the best I can to establish values and I feel satisfied with the results I'm seeing.

Add the numbers and divide by 5. If your score is 1–2.5, you are probably being an enemy to yourself in this area. If your score is 2.6–3.75, you may want to consider this area more to see what is fuzzy or what you could do to improve it. If your score is over 3.75, you are either strong in this area or partially blind, which may require a perspective of someone who knows you well.

Self-sabotage assessment: _____

Another person's assessment of me: _____

UNPACKING PROCEDURES

1. What seems to be the biggest challenge for you in establishing the right priorities?
2. How can you avoid this barrier?
3. List what you think are the top five values in your life. (What you say is worthwhile and enduring.)
   A.
   B.
   C.
   D.
   E.

4. List what you think are the top five priorities in your life, based on what you actually spend the most time doing.

   A.

   B.

   C.

   D.

   E.

5. Where do these two lists coincide? What is on one list that is not on the other?

6. Describe people you know who appear to have their priorities messed up (avoid using names if this is a group discussion). What results of this do you see?

7. Think of examples where you have put good and valuable things in front of the best and most valuable things. Any ideas on how to avoid this in the future?

Seven

HUNG BY THE TONGUE

How can she say that about me? That woman, she's wicked. After all the things I've done for her, I can't believe she would say that about me. She's such a two-faced hypocrite. She smiles at you and then as soon as you walk by, stabs you in the back. I never did trust her. She comes across like she's some kind of Goody Two-shoes, but I knew she wasn't as good as she acts. You think she's your friend, and then you find out that she's been telling everyone about your conversations. Honestly, what drives a woman to be that way? I knew she could talk, because she'd tell me about everyone else in our circle. Like I said, I trusted her. Some friend! You can't trust anyone these days. Well, two can play at this game. Maybe she'll be surprised when I let her friends know that she's colored her hair, had liposuction, and who knows what else. I'll fix her for letting her mouth run off. She is incredible!

Description and Dangers

Grandma was right: If you play with fire, you'll eventually get burned. Scripture warns us about the flammability of our words.

We all stumble in many ways. If anyone is never at fault in what he says, he is a perfect man, able to keep his whole body in check. . . . the tongue is a small part of the body, but it makes great boasts. Consider what a great forest is set on fire by a small spark. The tongue also is a fire, a world of evil among the parts of the body. It corrupts the whole person, sets the whole course of his life on fire, and is itself set on fire by hell.

All kinds of animals, birds, reptiles, and creatures of the sea are being tamed and have been tamed by man, but no man can tame the tongue. It is a restless evil, full of deadly poison.

With the tongue we praise our Lord and Father, and with it we curse men, who have been made in God's likeness. Out of the same mouth come praise and cursing. My brothers, this should not be. Can both fresh water and salt water flow from the same spring? My brothers, can a fig tree bear olives, or a grapevine bear figs? Neither can a salt spring produce fresh water.

James 3:2, 5–12

People cause more damage in what they say than the cumulative impact of natural disasters, bringing on themselves much unnecessary pain.

Do you have the following symptoms of being unable to control your tongue?

1. You say things that create tension in relationships and alienate people.
2. You speak with little forethought of how people will perceive what you say.
3. You have said things about people that got back to them and offended them.

The Danger of Not Recognizing the Impact of Words

Most people who engage in this behavitude are naive about the impact their words make. Satire, comical put-downs, and making someone else the butt of a joke may seem harmless but usually leave damaged emotions in their wake. Anyone who does a fair amount of counseling probably finds it difficult to enjoy Jay Leno's *Tonight Show* monologue, because so much of it pokes fun at other people. Those of us in the healing business realize how much ego pain results from such humor. Whenever we use words without thinking about their impact on others, we are in danger of piercing someone's heart.

The Danger of Gossip and Innuendo

The biggest single problem with gossip is that most people don't realize when they are doing it. They think it's innocent enough—offering their opinions (who can deny that right?), discussing a problem among friends (though the problem person is absent), and sharing a concern (which in church circles is a "prayer request").

For conversation to be considered gossip, there are distinct elements. First of all, the person being discussed is not present. Second, the discussion would change if the other person were present. Without these two characteristics, the conversation is not gossip.

Gossip is a way to get attention. People will listen to us because they tend to be voyeuristic, but if we continue the gossip habit, we find we've attracted the wrong kind of people. Those who are drawn to rumors and hearsay are people who do not have better goals to preoccupy their time. We're also telling people that we can't be trusted. When we talk about another person, we are silently telling our listener that if the situation arises, we will talk to others about him or her. Thus we may have attracted an audience but we've also created for ourselves an atmosphere of deception and distrust.

The Danger of Breached Confidence

"Loose lips sink ships" was a war slogan, urging people not to talk about military installations and wartime secrets. You never know who may be listening. When someone tells you something in official or unofficial confidence, it is both an honor and a burden. The honor is that the person trusted you with information that could be potentially embarrassing or damaging. The burden is that you now have to keep the secret. When you breach a confidence, you've jeopardized your relationship with the person who trusted you.

The Danger of Ill-Founded Opinions

Have you ever noticed how opinionated folks have become in recent years? Everyone has an opinion on nearly everything—restaurants, traffic, hairstyles, spouses, kids, others' spouses, others' kids, attire, temperature, movies, costs, on and on. The list is virtually endless. Before you give advice, share opinions, or make suggestions, be sure you've done some research. Know what you're talking about. When people discover that you're a know-it-all who really doesn't, you've shot yourself in the foot.

The Danger of Malice-Laced Anger

Malice-laced anger is a form of verbal destruction that hurts both the giver and the receiver. Healthy anger is a normal part of living. When we are angry over an injustice and especially when others are being hurt, it is righteous indignation. But most indignation is not righteous. While we may be justified in our frustration, we do damage when we make our anger a carrier for hate and character assassination. It is akin to putting barbs on a wire fence, creating barbed wire.

While healthy conflict resolution can be heated, it focuses on the situation, not on personalities. When we begin to attack and condemn people, we let our words become weapons instead of tools. Cutting remarks, verbal barbs, and snippets of defamation may seem like small darts but they produce significant damage. Angry comments tend to fester. The residual impact is immeasurable because we're not sure how many times other people will replay our words in their psyche—maybe once, perhaps a dozen times, or possibly an endless loop.

The Danger of Negativity

In our opinionated culture, a majority of our opinions are negative. That's because our human propensity is to notice what's wrong. We try to impress others with our good taste and eye for excellence by pointing out imperfections in everything—people, products, services. Our negative attitude may backfire, however, because people prefer to be around positive, hopeful people. Whatever our motive, our sour approach to life will turn people away.

The Danger of Alienating Ourselves from Others

Verbal abuse is self-defeating. It causes us to alienate the people we need in our life. To be whole people, we need others. We need them to fulfill things in us that cannot happen solo. But also it is essential for us to know that we are needed and wanted. Verbal fires lead to divorce, broken commitments, divided families, lost friendships, ruined jobs, bankruptcy, bodily injury, murder, and even national wars. When we say things that are not fully true or say true things in ways that can be easily misperceived, we become our own worst enemies.

The Danger of Ignoring Responsibility

The individual freedom we enjoy in America and most of Western society must be counterbalanced with responsibility for our actions and our words. The right to free speech is a defense against demagogy. Used irresponsibly, it becomes a tool for our own inner demise. Recognizing the power and value of words, our Founding Fathers made sure our speech was not squelched; so why do we not in turn understand how the misuse of our freedom to speak can undermine the moral fabric of our nation? Mismanagement of our mouths divides people. "United we stand. Divided we fall." Shame on us for accepting the constitutional right but rejecting the moral responsibility. Shame or no shame, we defeat ourselves when we choose to say things that end up causing us grief and problems. The prudent person comes to grips with the reality of verbal power.

The Danger of Being Uncovered

Our words are a window to our soul. What we say reflects who we are, which can be a negative thing if we are cynical, angry, and lack character. On our Midwest farm, we had window wells around our basement windows. These below-ground-level depressions allowed light into the basement and provided glimpses of the sky from within. Obviously, it also allowed you to look into the basement from outdoors. Consider your mouth a window well that allows you to get out what's in you for communication, problem solving, and brainstorming. Good or bad, it also provides the world a view of what's "down under." We cannot hide from what we say. It eventually reveals who we are.

Putting Our Foot in Our Mouth

Why are we careless about what we say when our words can hurt others and cause us pain and embarrassment? Here are four reasons:

1. *Talk is control.* Inherently people want control. This need to control is the essence of sin. The desire to be our own god and call the shots and make our own decisions according to our whims and wishes is the root of the problem. The sin behaviors that result are primarily symptomatic of our condition. While fruit gets our attention, root is the cause.

   When I was a boy, my dad would send me into the field to cut down thistle patches. Cutting thistles was hard work, so I learned an easy way to deal with them—hack them off at the stem. One day, I came back so early, my dad asked, "Did you get all the thistles?"

   "I did, Dad."

   The next week, driving through the field, he said to me, "I thought you said you cut all the thistles."

   "I did," I responded.

   He grabbed a shovel and said, "Come here. This is how you kill a thistle." He put the sharp edge of the pointed shovel below the surface of the ground and stepped on it, cutting the thistle off at the root. I had merely lopped off the tops above the surface of the ground, allowing them to grow back quickly. Lesson learned. Getting to the root of a matter is key.

   Speech is a very controlling medium. We use it to control other people, circumstances, perceptions, and spins on reality. Therefore, if we are to correct our corrupt tongues, we need to give up the need to control. Surrendering control to God is the critical first step that addresses the root of the problem.

2. *We have low self-esteem.* When people have low self-esteem, they are conditioned to see the negative in themselves. Then their mental filters will show other people and situations in a negative light. Generally people with low self-esteem are melancholy about relationships and life in general. Focusing on the weaknesses and negative traits in others, they tend to see others as some sort of threat. Thus, to defend themselves, they often use words as weapons, attacking potential enemies.

3. *We've never potty trained our mouths.* When I am in a writing mode, I tend to let something go—exercise. I do my work and take care of my family responsibilities (okay, maybe not the garage or closets), but I generally gain a few pounds and get flabby during a book crunch. My exercise discipline seems to disappear.

   Discipline is a pretty significant part of doing nearly everything in life that matters. As little children, we must learn that just because a body function comes naturally, it is not necessarily right to just let it go. Parents potty train their children, teaching them to recognize a natural function and to control it. Most of us learn this control as young children, and life becomes much more bearable for everyone concerned. We need to have the same kind of discipline for our mouth. Unfortunately many of us never learn that we don't have to let everything out that comes into our mind. Just as we learn to control our physical functions, we can learn control over what we say.

4. *We fail to consider the impact of our words.* Who can measure the weight of a word? Sometimes we are perplexed when people get offended, relationships go awry, and perceptions are skewed, but it's usually because we underestimated the weight of our words. Here are some questions to consider before speaking:

- Could I be easily misquoted?
- If I'm quoted or misquoted, is there anyone I would not want to hear this?
- Is this a confidential conversation?
- Are people hearing my real meaning or are my emotions telling them something different?
- Would I want my words to be read in tomorrow's newspaper?
- Would the person I'm talking about be offended by what I'm saying?

Becoming Your Own Best Ally

Don't Underestimate the Power of Words

Consider the echo effect. Words have a way of coming back to haunt us. Ask any politician. They have all learned how easy it is to be misquoted. We would all do better to hold our tongue. As someone said, better to be quiet and let people think you are a fool than to say something and remove all doubt. Usually people who speak less, but appropriately, are perceived to be wiser than those who talk a lot.

The problem with spoken words is how elusive they are. There's no way to prove what you really said, and words are impossible to take back. When you say something, who knows where it will end up and who will hear it? As soon as your words leave your mouth, they scatter, as though blown by the wind, to bring blessing or harm to the unsuspecting listener.

Don't Breathe Secondhand News

Scientists now tell us that secondhand smoke is as harmful or worse than our own smoking. The same is true of secondhand conversations. Context is everything. Communication experts say that without context, words have no meaning. You can try but you can never fully recreate context. "You should have been there" says it well. The attitude of the speaker, earlier and later conversations, and the emotional presentation all impact the actual words. You can quote a person word-for-word and still misquote him or her because you cannot recreate the context. Every time you make a copy of the copy, you lose clarity. So be careful about relating what someone else has said. Before quoting someone, consider the sensitivity of the message, the possibility of being misunderstood, and whether misrepresenting the person you are quoting would be harmful to him or her.

Learn the Nuances of Communication

Because communication is two-way, it is a matter of both what you say and how you are heard. When you say things while you are tired, angry, late, or generally stressed, you'll be prone to overcompensate in one area or more. Remember to underreact. Write a letter and then sleep on it. Take a chill pill. Count to ten. Go for a walk. Take a cold shower or hot bath. Walk, work out, or snooze a bit.

The other important factor in conversation is the mood of the receiver. Our ears play tricks on us when we're tired, angry, late, or generally stressed. When your spouse comes home after a difficult day on the job, it is not the time to talk about the check that bounced. Never confront another person via mail, e-mail, or an answering machine. You have no idea when the person will get your message, what kind of day the person has had, or how he or she will respond.

Be a Verbal Ecologist

Why do we think litter and pollution are merely physical manifestations? A verbal ecologist is a person who holds others accountable for their word littering. When you're with a group of people who are doing the old character assassination thing, affirm the positive in the person being discussed, turn the conversation to more constructive topics, suggest that it's not fair to talk about another person when he or she is not there to defend himself or herself, or just walk away. By turning your back on verbal littering, you are suggesting that it's not okay to junk the world. When you caringly confront polluters, you hold them responsible for their words.

Beware of the Listening Effect

During my study for my master's degree in communication-psychology at California State University, I learned this: "You cannot *not* communicate." Everything we do communicates something—what we say, don't say, spend, schedule, how we decorate, dress, and so on—are all saying something. While our focus here has primarily been about what we say, what we don't say is also a way to communicate. We can miscommunicate, even when we don't say a thing. For example, if you're listening to a person ramble on about his irritation with another person, your empathetic listening can be perceived to be agreement. Your silence and responsiveness may give the impression that the complainer is right and that you affirm what he says about the other person.

Learn Self-Discipline and Self-Denial

People who lack self-discipline tend to be loose with their tongue and wind up saying things they regret. The undisciplined person cannot be trusted. The story is told of three clergy in a meeting. The priest said, "I have a problem with drinking. Occasionally I drink too much of the ceremonial wine and get a little drunk."

The pastor responded, "You know, I have a problem with stealing. Sometimes I put my hand in the offering. I shouldn't do that either."

The third minister replied, "I have a problem with gossiping, and I can't wait to get out of this meeting."

Having the ability to hold your tongue shows self-discipline. Being quiet while others talk shows that you can deny yourself as you respect the rights and concerns of others. A rule of thumb for sharing a criticism is to do it only with someone who can help change the situation. Otherwise it is wasted energy. Self-discipline and self-denial can be fully achieved only when you pursue them using your spiritual resources.

Change the Inner Person

Sometimes in a sermon I illustrate the contents of our soul by holding up a sponge. I squeeze it and water drops onto the floor. Then I ask the audience, "Why did water come out of the sponge?" The typical first response is, "Because you squeezed it." The right answer is, "Because water was in the sponge." If I had squeezed the sponge and milk or oil or paint was in the sponge, water wouldn't come out. Consider the water faucet in your kitchen sink. When you turn the faucet handle, whatever is in the pipes comes out of the spout. Imagine that your mouth is a water spout. When you open the valve (speak), whatever comes out is an indicator of what's inside of you.

Although you can strive to build in all sorts of screens, valves, and checks and balances, the surest way to control your verbal outflow is to change the reservoir. When you're full of faith, hope, and love, no matter how much you're squeezed from the outside, only what is constructive and positive will emerge. The human approach is to work at being disciplined. The spiritual approach is to become a different person from the inside out.

SELF-SABOTAGE ASSESSMENT

Place a value of 1 to 5 in the box beside each statement: 1 = no/rarely 2 = infrequently 3 = sometimes 4 = usually 5 = yes/always

☐ 1. I can keep from telling a secret.
☐ 2. People avoid telling me their gossip.
☐ 3. I am consistently positive about other people, regardless of what others are saying.
☐ 4. People mention how positive I am.
☐ 5. I share my criticisms only with people who can help change the situation.

Add the numbers and divide by 5. If your score is 1–2.5, you are probably being an enemy to yourself in this area. If your score is 2.6–3.75, you may want to consider this area more to see what is fuzzy or what you could do to improve it. If your score is over 3.75, you are either strong in this area or partially blind, which may require a perspective of someone who knows you well.

Self-sabotage assessment: _____

Another person's assessment of me: _____

UNPACKING PROCEDURES

1. Describe a person you know who is quite a gossip. Why do you think this person behaves this way?

2. What are some ways you can avoid entering into gossip? How can you let others know that you consider gossip off-limits?
3. Describe a time when something you said created a lot of pain for you.
4. Think of someone you know who is incredibly positive and does not cut down others. What can you learn from him or her about how to behave this way?
5. Describe a time when you were hurt by another person who said something about you behind your back. How could this person have dealt with the situation differently?
6. How can you begin to implement the principles of this chapter and avoid defeating yourself with what you say?

Eight

I CAN'T SAY NO

I'm not a derelict. I hold down a good job, have never been arrested, and pay my taxes. But I also like to enjoy life, you know, live it up a little. Sometimes, though, I have a hard time setting limits—like last night. Ughhh, I wish I hadn't gone to that party. My friends invited me and when I thought it best that I not go, they harassed me into submission. Then I had a little too much to drink and said some things that I'm embarrassed to think about right now. I have to make a couple of apology calls. I hate doing that. Who knows what else I did that made me look like a jerk? My life's a mess. I'm out of shape, eat too much, let the bills stack up too high, not to mention the laundry. There are so many opportunities to have fun, go places, spend money, and I have so little willpower.

Description and Dangers

We've all been there, that deserted island called *regret*. It's no resort in the vacation sense of the term, but we resort to it far too often, because of our inability to say no. The reason we feel alone is because the result of not saying no at strategic times creates personal remorse. Often we hear people say things like, "I could kick myself for . . ."

"I can't believe I let him talk me into . . ." "Why didn't I just say no?"

There are two primary issues behind these regrets. One is a matter of judgment, the other of self-discipline. When you see a person who consistently expresses a lack of good judgment, you may feel sad. This person brings on so much of his or her pain because of poor choices. While training and a willingness to learn may help, some people seem predestined to a life of problems because of poor decision-making.

The other issue has to do with power versus steering. Your car may be headed in the right direction, but if you don't have an engine under the hood, you're destined to go nowhere. You'll be easy prey for the multitude of tow trucks, offering you a lift to who knows where. Just because someone makes you an offer doesn't mean you have to accept it.

Do you have the following symptoms of being unable to say no?

1. You feel bad turning down door-to-door salesmen and/or phone solicitors.
2. You commonly say yes when people ask a favor and later you regret it.
3. You have a difficult time setting limits and are often frustrated by a lack of self-discipline.

The Danger of Imbalance

Few of us can be consistently disciplined in all areas all the time. We heap guilt on ourselves for not being able to do it all—exercise, have quiet time, keep the house clean, mow the yard, run the kids to sports, date our mate, work, and balance the checkbook. Chances are slim we can do all of this daily. But we can shoot for weekly balance. Trying to cover the necessary bases on a weekly schedule provides a greater opportunity to accomplish our goals before we give up in frustration. If we are unable to say no to interruptions, the temptation to procrastinate, and people pushing their agendas on us, we will look back at few accomplishments and numerous regrets.

People can also be too disciplined, always saying no to any temptation to deviate from their schedule. Losing sight of their original goal, they make self-discipline an obsession. They subconsciously come to revere the art of self-discipline even more than whatever it is they are using the discipline to achieve, and the feeling of being in control becomes more important than achieving more meaningful goals. The neurotic need for order and control is at times an overcompensation for fear, feeling out of control, and self-esteem issues.

The Danger of Diminished Self-esteem

When we can't say no and we give into temptation, we can build up a guilt complex. When that happens time after time, we are prone to give up. Defeat nags at our self-esteem. We say to ourselves, *What's the use? Why do I even try? I'm a loser.* The person trying to lose weight feels depressed after bingeing at an all-you-can-eat buffet. The woman yearning for affection, who gives her body away as a means to get it, feels cheapened and used. The spendthrift who exhausts the savings account is miserable amidst the bags of new purchases.

Whenever we compromise morally, it tears at our self-image. We were created in the image of God and the residual of that image is an unconscious knowledge that we need to do what is right. The word *righteousness* sounds very theological, but actually it is best defined as "right-use-ness." The right-use-ness of our bodies, souls, minds, attitudes, and resources is what the Bible is about. The inability to say no to the wrong things tarnishes us.

The Danger of Saying Yes Inappropriately

I am told that one of the main reasons for starvation in India has to do with the Hindu belief in reincarnation. All the animals are left untouched and may eat the grain, even though they take precious supplies from people. In a similar fashion, when we let other people, invitations, or opportunities devour our resources, we are weakened. Then we are unable to say yes to opportunities that come our way that are truly valuable or interest us, because we're already committed, overextended, or just too busy. The danger of settling for less over the long haul is not just the potential we ignore. Stories abound about people who regret quickly saying yes to an offer, because it prevented them from saying yes to a better offer that came along later.

The Danger of Fewer Positive Relationships

Respect is something that must be earned. We usually like being around people we respect, who are loving, fun, and stimulating. When we lack self-discipline and are unable to say no appropriately, others will probably not respect us. They may endure, patronize, and even commit to us, but our lack of self-discipline will strain many of our relationships. When our friends and family members do not respect us, our relationships with them will not meet our needs.

Unable to Say No

Why don't we say no to things that will be bad for us? Here are four reasons:

1. *Our self-esteem is based on being liked and accepted by another person.* When we depend on being liked and accepted by others to feel good about ourselves, we

will have a hard time saying no to things they want us to do. When people ask us to do something—anything from joining a youth gang, to selling a product, to going out on the town with friends—they do not always have our welfare in mind. In that heat of the moment, we're apt to do nearly anything that the group tells us to do, if our value is based on how others accept us.

The inverse is true as well. Sometimes the self-esteem of others depends on our yes. My grandmother was a wonderful woman, but like other women of her generation, she identified her self-worth with her cooking. If you did not take a healthy first serving of a dish, let alone second and third helpings, you got the feeling you had offended her. When another person's self-esteem is based on our yes, our saying no tests our own sense of security. When our security is based on how another person responds to us, we're likely to say or do whatever generates a positive response, regardless of our opinions. When we are secure apart from others, we are freer to do what we think is right.

2. *We confuse saying yes to a person with accepting and affirming him or her.* You can accept another person without necessarily agreeing with everything he or she says. When we confuse this, we think that we need to make someone else happy and agree to whatever it is he or she is requesting. If we say no, the other person may have hurt feelings, quit the job, reject us, or retaliate. We let them pull our strings because we've misunderstood our responsibility to love. People who love us only when we say yes to them are not apt to be the kind of friends we need or want.

3. *We've failed to exercise a strong self-discipline muscle or practice delayed gratification.* When we're out of shape physically, we tire more easily, have less stamina, and have less strength. When we're out of shape emotionally,

our self-discipline may founder because self-discipline is a decision muscle. When it is weak, it is very difficult for us to delay gratification. We want what we want now. We are vulnerable because the more we buy into instant gratification, the more difficult it is to delay it, and a vicious cycle gains momentum.

When we learn how to delay gratification, we are apt to be more disciplined. If self-denial is a stranger, however, we tend to ignore it, thus avoiding the benefits of this potential friend.

4. *We have not adopted an internal set of standards, which provides a moral and ethical decision track.* As a youth pastor, I taught my adolescent parish that the time to decide on sexual standards is before you are in the backseat of a car. In the midst of a pressured decision, very few of us have the ability to take a time-out, weigh the moral elements, and determine what we ought to do. Just as it is advantageous to go into an auction knowing what your spending limit is, it is beneficial to know what you will and will not do before you are in a position to make a choice. This allows you to respond quickly, appropriately, and with confidence, based on predetermined standards. Making your standards up as you go results in low standards and eventual regrets. Although you can adopt someone else's standards, you'll do better to take ownership of your own. You'll be more committed to standards that you've determined are worth holding.

Becoming Your Own Best Ally

Practice Self-discipline

No Olympic weight lifter began his career pumping a world record. He started the same way we all start, with light weights. You have to begin small. Because your self-discipline or ability to say no is an inner muscle, it will be weak without training. Develop a regimen for yourself so you can get some wins under your belt. You could begin by going to the mailbox and saying no to every advertisement that's there. Talk back to your radio or TV when it wants to sell you something. The goal is not to go crazy or become malicious but to experience self-denial and others-denial in small doses. If your inability to say no has moral implications, such as sex outside of marriage, gossip, pornography, lying, stealing, or shady business dealings, then spend time feeding your moral muscle as well. Scripture reading, going to church, listening to Christian tapes, and hanging out with people who model morality are practical ways to reinforce moral boundaries.

Hang around Moral People

No one is an island. We are influenced positively or negatively by those around us. Although the essence of this book is affirming our responsibility for our own actions, we can make it easier on ourselves if we intentionally strive to be around people who will be a good example and who won't compromise our standards. Setting yourself up for failure, especially if your ability to say no is weak, is ridiculous.

Recovery groups are great places to find extra help among peers who struggle in specific areas. Finding a sponsor for support and accountability will provide positive peer pressure in your quest for self-control. This is basic to the philosophy of Alcoholics Anonymous. Another fundamental key behind the AA movement is the realization that you can't correct your faults by yourself. You need the help of "a higher power." While you can find moral folks wherever you look, your batting average is apt to improve when you hang around churches and faith communities, which study and practice moral guides like the Bible.

Put Each Decision on Pause

To make a wise decision, it is necessary to prethink potential outcomes and to remove yourself from the emotional pressure of the moment. Hit the snooze button. Most of the time, when we can't say no, we are heeding our hormones and/or being propelled by our feelings of the moment. Emotions are fleeting and can play tricks on us. If we live according to our emotions, our lives will be on a constant roller coaster. I remember the story of a young woman who was weary from drugs and a promiscuous lifestyle. She was at the brink of giving up. In desperation she walked into a church and met with a pastor. She realized that her lifestyle was killing her, but she began to regain hope as she confessed her failures. She said, "You mean, I don't have to do what I want to do?"

You don't. Your body is not in charge. Your hormones are not the boss. You are not a slave to your emotions. Defer the craving. Put the decision on hold. Procrastinate the yes so that you can build up strength to say the no.

Invest Time with God

Self-discipline is not just a home-cooked cure for our inability to say no. It's a part of our inner core, our spiritual being. While emotional intelligence and spiritual intelligence are not the same, there are certain things that a spiritual emphasis brings to life. "For God did not give us a spirit of timidity, but a spirit of power, of love and of self-discipline" (2 Tim. 1:7). Self-love and self-discipline go hand in hand.

Self-esteem is little more than a psychological term for recognizing God's love for us. Parents who love their children say no sometimes—and occasionally a lot. They do not let their children eat whatever they want, go to bed whenever they want, or hang out with whomever they want. They help them learn what is right and wrong, healthy and unhealthy.

When we invest time with our Creator, we gain similar direction and inner fortitude to say no to what is not good for us. Hungry souls are easily swayed, but inner strength produces proper inner direction. Muscle without wisdom does little good. Wisdom without muscle is useless.

SELF-SABOTAGE ASSESSMENT

Place a value of 1 to 5 in the box beside each statement: 1 = no/rarely 2 = infrequently 3 = sometimes 4 = usually 5 = yes/always

- [ ] 1. I feel comfortable saying no to a friend when I don't feel like doing what he or she suggests.
- [ ] 2. When I say no to a friend, I do not linger long on my response and feel guilty for not saying yes.
- [ ] 3. I am able to say no to urges without pondering them long.
- [ ] 4. I am disciplined in my lifestyle.
- [ ] 5. I have a predetermined set of ethics and morals that guides me in my decision-making on a regular basis.

Add the numbers and divide by 5. If your score is 1–2.5, you are probably being an enemy to yourself in this area. If your score is 2.6–3.75, you may want to consider this area more to see what is fuzzy or what you could do to improve it. If your score is over 3.75, you are either strong in this area or partially blind, which may require a perspective of someone who knows you well.

Self-sabotage assessment: _____

Another person's assessment of me: _____

UNPACKING PROCEDURES

1. What is the area you are weakest in regarding self-discipline and the ability to say no?
2. What is an area where you are self-disciplined and saying no is not a problem?
3. To whom do you have the most difficult time saying no?
4. Think of someone who is very disciplined, to the point that he or she is no fun and is overly controlled.
5. Think of someone who is very undisciplined. How has his or her inability to say no created problems for him or her?
6. What do you do to strengthen your inner spiritual muscle? How does this affect your decision-making and willpower?

Nine

HAVE BAGS, WILL TRAVEL

The scenario was all too familiar. John and Carol came to our church after seeing the street signs and hearing about it from their neighbors. They grew up going to church but quit after they left home for college. John and Carol knew they were missing something. Life had been good to them, but they didn't feel fulfilled. So they came for a trial visit, kids in tow. They liked what they experienced and returned again and again.

Both John and Carol began to grow, and their lives were changing. But suddenly their attitudes seemed different. It was hard to explain. Because their growth had become deeper and more challenging, they began to wonder if they could keep it up. Their church attendance became more and more sporadic. Then one Sunday, they approached me.

"Well, Pastor, we've decided to switch churches. Thanks for all you've done for us. We appreciate your hard work and ministry. It's nothing personal, but we just feel like we need something else. We're going to look around at some other churches to see if we can find one that's right for us. Even though we haven't been here very long, and we haven't gotten that involved, we think it's time to go. We'll keep in touch."

John and Carol didn't keep in touch. They also never found another church. Instead they stopped going to church and returned to their previous lifestyle.

Description and Dangers

Whenever a group of pastors gets together, the topic of the front-door/back-door mobility of their congregations comes up. One pastor, who's been at his church for thirty-five years, was asked the secret for his longevity. "Well, I figured that either I could move every three to four years, or the families in my church could move every three to four years, and I figured it was easier on my family if we stayed in one place."

The interesting thing is that this rolling-stone phenomenon is not unique to congregations. Our mobile society has the mind-set that growing roots is bad and staying on the move is good.

I remember driving cross-country through Kansas. To stay awake, I tried to run over tumbleweeds that blew across the highway. Tumbleweed people move from job to job, church to church, house to house, and friend to friend. Mortgage bankers benefit from our mobility. Although the typical home mortgage is amortized over thirty years, most homeowners keep their loans only three to five years, so the banks make extra profit in origination fees. Mobility has become a scapegoat for all sorts of weak-kneed commitments and cowardly escapes. Unfortunately our attempts to find greener grass and to keep our options open end up sabotaging what we could be experiencing in life.

Given the mobility of our society, due to transfers, takeovers, mergers, and right-sizing, sinking roots can be difficult. The necessity to seek adequate employment is not always the same as seeking greener grass. At times there is a fine line between chronic dissatisfaction and desiring growth and improvement. When God leads, we must follow. When he does not, we would do best to check our motives and inner drives.

Do you have the following symptoms of being unable to stay put?

1. You change jobs, churches, and/or houses every two to four years.
2. You have not seen long-term fruit from your labor because you've never been in one place long-term.
3. You are consistently restless where you are, thinking things are better in some other place.

The Danger of Moving on Too Quickly

Every spring we planted crops. With the proper moisture, fertilizer, and cultivation, we could expect a bountiful harvest. If we put the corn seed in the ground in April, my father did not walk into the field in June and say, "Well, I don't see any ears of corn on these stalks. Apparently, my hard work and huge investment haven't paid off, so I'm plowing it all under." That would be a foolish thing to do. Obviously he waited until fall for the crop to fully mature.

A chef does not turn off the oven when the meal is half done. Even microwaves take some time to cook. Far too often we lose patience with the process and quit too soon, missing out on what we could have gained. In these fast times, we run the risk of cutting short the harvest. Watching the corn grow can be a very anxious process. We want it safely in the barn now. Yesterday would be even better.

Our lives are one big hurry. We rush through our childhood, red lights, and lovemaking as if channel surfing. We speed-read directions, come late to and leave early from meetings, and choose a church because its worship service is precisely one hour long. Our addiction to speed gets us things we'd not have without it, but it also guarantees we'll never see things we long for most. For example, going into debt to purchase a car, clothes, and vacation can keep us from qualifying for a house or the kind of home we dream about. Haste in a relationship can ruin long-term fulfillment, because we go too fast too soon or wind up with someone who is less than our dreams. The unwillingness to persevere with an organization through its trying times can cut us out of potential rewards when the tide changes. Waiting for the harvest is not fun for most of us, but when we plant seed and then run off to some other plot of ground without reaping our harvest, we've wasted a portion of our lives.

The Danger of Instant Living

If you live with the mind-set that things must happen instantaneously, you can achieve a lot. Many things can be gained with short-term, on-the-go action. But there is a whole other set of accomplishments that come only with time. Remember, a mushroom grows in a day but an oak tree takes many years. It depends on what you want. If you want everything in a hurry, you automatically exclude yourself from the things that come only with time.

Much of life can't be rushed, especially the things that matter most, such as character, intimacy, and wisdom. These qualities cannot be suddenly adopted or learned in a classroom. Most wisdom is not gleaned from books but is ours only after many varied experiences and struggles.

In this age of microprocessors, we tend to think that everything can be ours instantaneously, so we try to rush our kids into adulthood, our spouses into perfection, and our work into success. But maturity and perfection and, often, success are like the Grand Canyon. They don't happen overnight and no amount of technology will make them come faster. When we invest time and effort in worthwhile things, we are investing wisely.

The Danger of Pulling into Ourselves

There's a danger that, in our rush through life, we will pull into ourselves emotionally, never letting others get to know us because we're on the move. Being efficient at work is commendable, but being efficient with people doesn't produce lasting relationships, which require effectiveness. You can't speed-read your kids. They rebel against it. When you jump to conclusions with your spouse, you'll ruin intimacy.

Relationships and people take time, so we are prone to avoiding them because of our transient lifestyles. Staying superficial saves us from the pain that comes from broken relationships. Many of us live around people without knowing their names or what they do for a living. Our interactions are guarded, superficial, and plastic: "The lawyer next door bought a new car. Must be doing well. Saw the moving van in front of the house across the street. Wonder where they're going. The house a block over just went on the market. What are they asking for it?" Just as coastal locals prepare for a hurricane by closing the shutters and nailing up doors, we protect ourselves emotionally by boarding up our souls. Stranded inside our fortresses, we refuse to let others get to know us so that we don't get hurt when one of us has to pull out after just a few months in the hood.

The Danger of Hurting Others

If each of us were an island in society, we could pretty much mess up our own life without affecting others. Good or bad, that's not the way things work. When we drag around family members as we move from place to place, we steal from them childhood memories, a sense of security, their own friendships, and even part of their identity. When we pull out of a church, we leave a ministry vacuum (if we've gotten involved), financial hurt (if we've given), disappointed friends (assuming we've made some), and unanswered concerns. When we leave as leaders, we potentially damage the organization, hoping it will find someone as good as or better than us. When we leave as employees, we burden our teammates and lower productivity.

Moving around causes stress on our family members. This stress can create in turn unnecessary marital and family tension. I've counseled dozens of individuals who have been damaged by one person's unending need to move on. Each transition results in a trail of challenges.

While looking for that optimum situation, we underestimate what each move is costing us and our family. By trying to find what we're missing, we end up losing the benefits of stability and longevity. When we hurt those around us, we hurt ourselves as well.

Avoiding Roots

Why do we move around so much when it's self-defeating? Here are four reasons:

1. *We buy into the greener grass myth, confusing roots with ruts.* I saw this phenomenon occasionally on the farm. There would be two pastures separated by a fence. Occasionally I would see cows on opposite sides of the fence, reaching through the wire to eat grass on the other side. Each cow seemed to think the grass on the other side of the fence was better eating. We're no different. Kids, teens, and adults all suffer from the greener grass syndrome. Everything looks better in the store window, on someone else, or in another person's living room.

   When we allow ourselves to get involved in relationships, work, or life in general, we realize there are troubles. There is no perfect job, spouse, child, parent, school, or church. We are forever looking at the options, as if the perfect exists somewhere else. When we see something that looks better on the outside than what we have, we trade. We give up what we have to pursue the new thing. More times than not, we are discouraged to discover that the greener grass still needs to be mowed, watered, fertilized, and weeded.

2. *We are afraid of succeeding.* Fears come in all shapes and sizes. One of the most common is the fear of success. While we seem to yearn for it with all our heart, we are also leery of it because of what it will require of us. Success is difficult to maintain. "I don't deserve it. I'm not sure that I can handle the responsibility. I'm really a loser." So we sabotage ourselves. We do something that will mess up the machinery. Of course, one way to avoid success is to keep moving before the harvest. We then justify why we've not reached the level of success that we claim to desire. We create an alibi for our lack of productivity.

3. *We don't want to develop lasting relationships when we would have to work through significant life issues.* Churches are basically in the people-building business. Someone will start attending a church and begin growing. The initial growth is exciting and stimulating. The person gleams with enthusiasm as he or she sees behaviors and attitudes beginning to change and fruit being produced. But along the growth path, the person comes up against barriers that must be removed if he or she is to grow further. When the person is unwilling to let go and/or confront the barrier, he or she will retreat and growth stops. This is another dilemma, though, because in growth-oriented cultures, it is uncomfortable to stay as you are.

Soul-growth centers (local churches), doing their job, do not condemn but they do encourage our growth through their various programs, events, and services. So, to avoid significant growth, we have to run. We leave people who confront us about our baggage. We cut off those who remind us of where we're weak. By hitting the road, however, we hurt ourselves. We never work through growth issues and this retards our maturity.

4. *We've been hurt in the past and we want to avoid future pain.* Past hurts come back to haunt us in many ways. If we have been injured by someone who left us, or were betrayed by a confidant, we are prone to avoid similar situations in the future. By staying on the move, we never let people get to know us well enough to hurt us. When we spend time with people, they learn about our strengths and weaknesses. But weaknesses can be used to defeat us. We can lose respect, pride, and acceptance. People can take advantage of our known weaknesses. If we remain guarded and change the locks on our doors every so often, our secrets stay with us. No one can use them to hurt us. Unfortunately, while we keep out potential hurt, we also avoid possible love. By remaining anonymous for too long, we damage our emotions for lack of intimacy and friendship. When fear becomes a primary motivation, we are bound to have regrets. Sometimes we are not aware of this, but our subconscious fear of pain keeps us moving.

Becoming Your Own Best Ally

Put Down Roots and Grow

After a few moves, you should have a feel for what fits you and what you're looking for. If you do not, it means you're not learning along the way and/or you're probably running from something. I know many people who at midlife choose not to work up the ranks of the company because it requires a relocation. The challenge of buying and selling a house, in addition to the stress on children, friends, and marriage, is not worth the tangible rewards of a promotion. After a while, you begin to recognize what you want. You see things that money cannot buy and when you find them, you do what it takes to keep them. More and more, you can do this with telecommuting, self-employment, and e-commerce, avoiding the need to make a move. Do not buy into the idea that you have to keep relocating to accomplish your dreams in life. And don't let a perfectionistic attitude ruin every place you go.

When people attend our church, we sometimes tell them up front that this is not a perfect church with perfect people or a perfect pastor. And if you ever find a perfect congregation, don't join it, because when you do, it won't be perfect anymore.

List some nonessentials in life that are important to you. Consider yourself fortunate if you have realized these. Some people are impossible to please and they are forever critical wherever they go, ruining their own enjoyment and the joy of those around them.

Get Involved

Plug in where you're at as if it were for the long term. You may not have the option of telling your family, "We're not going to move again." Maybe you are uncertain about your company or what you'll be doing in ten years. But you can live as if you're going to be at a place long term. After a few moves, most people become emotionally guarded, avoiding relationships, not redecorating their house, and intentionally keeping to themselves. This mind-set ruins life wherever you go. As soon as you call a place home, begin establishing relationships and life as you desire it from that location. Leaving the pictures in the boxes and avoiding church, school, and community involvement guarantee a sterile existence. Take the plunge. Jump in. Make friends and be vulnerable. Life is too short to alienate yourself. It's amazing how little time it takes to feel at home and see positive results when you decide to get involved right away. Volunteer at your church and school. Take a plate of cookies around to your neighbors; don't wait for them to extend a welcome. Get to know the grocery store clerks by name. These are just a few examples of living as if you're a long-termer, even if you can't guarantee longevity.

Confront the Issues

If you discover that you're a tumbleweed person, you will want to dig deeper to discover the cause for your aversion to staying in any one place too long. Perhaps as a child you never saw commitment modeled. Maybe you are fearful of being found out or that people will leave you after you get close to them. Leaving others puts you in the driver's seat in some ways.

Buried reasons, as well as those on the surface, motivate us to do what we do. If you're easily bored, never satisfied, and constantly seeking greener grass, it may be more than just "how you're wired." You may be avoiding something. If you have a problem with people and offend many after a year or two, unable to make things right, you'll forever be running. Instead of confronting inadequate people skills, you keep replenishing your supply of people. It's like water leaking in a broken toilet. You pay the water bills instead of fixing the plumbing. When we fail to confront unhealthiness in our lives, we take our problems with us wherever we go. This means we'll forever be plagued with a desire to move because we carry our baggage with us to each new location.

Benefits of Long-term Commitments

When you're anxious about staying in one place, concentrate on the good things that happen only as a result of time. Seeing your house appreciate; eliminating the stress of locating new shopping resources, doctors, and schools; letting the kids build memories; and seeing friendships deepen are all pluses that only time will provide. Getting to know your way around a community and what it has to offer takes time. Becoming familiar with your surroundings so that you can appreciate what you have at your disposal takes effort.

We fantasize about the Mayberry RFD small-town feel or the relational communities we see in the sitcoms *Cheers, Seinfeld,* or *Friends.* These can be experienced in part when you put down roots. There are some things you'll never experience in life without long-term commitment. Stopping to consider what you'll be losing if you pick up and leave helps you persevere through the periods of conflict, boredom, and anxiety. Unpack your bags and boxes. Stay a while. Welcome home.

SELF-SABOTAGE ASSESSMENT

Place a value of 1 to 5 in the box beside each statement: 1 = no/rarely 2 = infrequently 3 = sometimes 4 = usually 5 = yes/always

☐ 1. I have lived in my house and attended the same faith community for more than five years.

☐ 2. I try to sink roots as soon as possible after a move.

☐ 3. I have stayed in one job more than five years.
☐ 4. I get excited about staying in one place more than five years.
☐ 5. I make long-term commitments.

Add the numbers and divide by 5. If your score is 1–2.5, you are probably being an enemy to yourself in this area. If your score is 2.6–3.75, you may want to consider this area more to see what is fuzzy or what you could do to improve it. If your score is over 3.75, you are either strong in this area or partially blind, which may require a perspective of someone who knows you well.

Self-sabotage assessment: _____

Another person's assessment of me: _____

UNPACKING PROCEDURES

1. Why do you think people move around so much?
2. What are the positives about new moves? What are the negatives?
3. Why did you leave your last church?
4. Why did you leave your last job?
5. Why did you leave your last neighborhood?
6. What is keeping you from making long-term commitments?
7. How can you establish roots in today's world without losing out on opportunities that require major changes?

Ten

LOOK, MOM, NO HANDS

"I do it for *you*," Keith said. "I can't believe how little you appreciate my hard work. I work fifty hours per week and took on a part-time job to provide for my family. You're spoiled. You don't even care how much I break my back for you."

"Honey," Sarah, his wife, responded. "It's not that we don't appreciate all you do for us. It's just that we want *you*, not new carpet or a bigger house. We're happy with what we have. The kids just want to spend time with you."

"How can you say that?" Keith asked. "Braces, sports, new clothes, vacations, and a car that is dependable—someone has to provide for these."

"Keith, it's not that we don't want some of these, but we could do with less. It's like you're worried about impressing the neighbors or your dad or whoever. Keeping up with the Joneses seems like an obsession with you. If we have all these things but never see you, what good are they?"

"So what am I supposed to do? I can't please anyone. I feel like giving up," Keith said in desperation.

Description and Dangers

Children love to please their parents. They constantly seek attention, affirmation, and acceptance. The little boy who is not satisfied with merely riding his bicycle for his mom shows off by riding past the front yard with both hands in the air, "Look, Mom, no hands." One more feat, one more accomplishment, and still another opportunity to impress a significant other.

The burden to please or impress others can be overwhelming. It can cause us to mortgage our lives to the hilt and compromise our self-worth in the process. People-pleasing is the inverse of the self-sabotaging behavitude that others should make *you* happy. If you believe that your job in life is to make others happy or at least to impress them, you suffer from the behavitude of always trying to please others. If at first you do not accomplish this, you try longer and harder. Then if you get unsatisfactory responses, you become frustrated and even depressed. You shoulder the negative emotions of others, as if you are able to flip the inner switch that is under their control. The inability to control the attitudes and behaviors of others is enough to drive a people-pleaser nuts. The need to make people happy appears pious and altruistic, but it destines a person to a life filled with anxiety and disappointment.

Do you have the following symptoms of trying to please or impress everyone around you?

1. You have a strong desire to please people, feeling responsible for the happiness of others.
2. You feel hurt and worry excessively when you think people are unhappy because of something you did or did not do.
3. You exhibit workaholic tendencies, created by over-achieving, motivated by trying to impress others.

The Danger of Setting Ourselves Up to Fail

The reason this behavitude is self-defeating is because we are basing our joy and fulfillment on our ability to make other people happy. As we've learned, happiness is an inside job. We can influence but cannot ultimately determine a specific response in others. Lacking control of others, we are set up for failure. Overconcern about the well-being and fulfillment of others tends to work against us. We begin to get stressed out with trying to impress and please people, which in turn puts a strain on the very relationships we want to enhance. We feel taken advantage of because at times we are.

The Danger of Attaching Strings to Our Love

If you think about it, most people don't give love, they trade it. *I love you when, if, because, and in order to* . . . are all common attachments that distort true love. We exchange favors. You be nice to me and I'll be nice to you. It's a way of doing business, appearing to be wonderful human beings even though it is a shallow sort of love.

When we attach strings to our love, we cease to love others based on their personal value as human beings. Instead, we make our love dependent on their actions or, worse, on our perceptions and opinions of their actions. This kind of roller-coaster relating creates all sorts of strange and dysfunctional symptoms. We are more or less victims of our own making because we try to control others by harnessing them to our love. As a result, every relationship runs the risk of imploding and lacks the integrity of mature, meaningful love.

The Danger of Workaholism

Workaholism is a common phenomenon in our fast-paced world. It's not always in response to competition, survival of the fittest, or even a joy of productivity. A motivational mutation behind work addiction is the need to succeed to win the affirmation of a significant other, past or present. By proving that we really do amount to something, we strive to affirm our worth to a parent, spouse, or critical sibling. Obviously, when we work harder and longer than our peers, there is a good chance that we will outperform them, get a bigger bonus, and climb the ladder at a faster pace. If we could clone ourselves, we could really excel. Workaholism is an attempt to clone ourselves by doing a little bit more than would normally be expected of one person. By winning the admiration and applause of a selective society, we achieve what we believe will bring us satisfaction.

The Danger of Relying on Others' Responses

Behind an approval-hungry heart is a person who bases his or her worth on the responses of others. I hope that you are beginning to see that our self-image and self-worth play a part in many of these behavitudes. This is because how we see ourselves and what we base our worth on are primary motivators throughout life. To merely suggest that a lack of sufficient esteem is our sole problem would be overly simplistic and not very helpful. Seeing the many ways inadequate self-esteem displays itself gives us a better idea of its subtlety and how to address the problem.

When we lack perceived inner worth, we are relying on the external strokes we get from others. By pleasing and impressing them, we are more apt to obtain those strokes, which make us feel good about ourselves, at least temporarily. By constantly manufacturing good deeds, sexual attractiveness (beauty), and accomplishments, we stand a good chance of harvesting the admiration and appreciation we seek. The problem is that this kind of behavior is emotionally taxing and reduces us to selling ourselves to others.

The Pleasing-People Trap

Why are we so concerned with pleasing others when it is self-defeating? Here are four reasons:

1. *We confuse pleasing people with loving people.* At times pleasing people and loving people are the same, but at other times they are not. Sometimes love must be tough. It must do things that create discomfort, perceived neglect, and delayed gratification. Many who have had a loved one struggling with an addictive habit know that the desire to please often conflicts with the need to love. Those who are unwilling to endure the pain of being misunderstood by the loved one often cave in and do what will bring pleasure to that person. But the fulfillment is often short-lived and ultimately digs the person deeper into his or her hole. Sometimes love is pleasing, but sometimes it is not. Sometimes pleasing is loving, but sometimes it is not.

2. *We expect people to please us in return. Trading love* is perhaps the most common form of love. *Giving love* expects nothing in return. We all hope for love, enjoy it, and desire it, but expecting and demanding it of others fouls up a good relationship.

   Some of the most effective people-pleasers are actually those who rely on others for their happiness. They have discovered that people are more apt to make them happy if they first or at the same time strive to make other people happy. This reciprocity often pays off. As a general rule, it appears to be an unselfish approach to achieving our needs. "You scratch my back, I'll scratch yours. I'll make you happy so you'll make me happy." The inherent problem with this motivation is that it is not unselfish and when people do not reciprocate, we feel taken advantage of, become resentful, and end up withdrawing our "love" from the other person. This of course strains a relationship that could otherwise be fruitful. This *trading love* really is a smoke screen, creating the appearance that we are truly loving when in reality we are just using our love to get the love we need.

3. *We've not outgrown the need for the affirmation and approval of others, what I call external love.* My wife and I have three sons. We know as parents how much kids want the attention and affirmation of Mom and Dad. Someone suggested we should have only two kids. We agreed, but God decided he wanted us to have a third (at least we blamed God). We love our three boys immensely, but the odd number can be overwhelming at times. When there is one parent per child, you can pretty much handle the need for attention when it arises, but there is something about three that changes the whole chemistry. Sometimes when we're driving in the van, all three want attention at once and begin their informal competition, which can only be compared to a feeding frenzy of famished fish. My wife fares much better than I do in these situations. She seems unruffled by conversing with three kids in overlapping stories, questions, and requests. She tells me it's because I'm an only child. Regardless, a child's need for demonstrations of love is obvious.

Somewhere between childhood and adulthood, there should come a transition where we are able to sustain our self-worth through internal versus external love. From a theological angle, *self-esteem* (inner love) is another term for recognizing God's love for us. When this is established, we enjoy but do not require outside acts of love to verify our self-worth. Just as adults learn to feed, bathe, and clothe themselves, emotional adults are able to maintain their own sense of value. Like making the switch from battery power to AC, we must learn to connect directly to the power source within. External love, like batteries, eventually lets us down. Wanting affirmation is fine, but when our emotional state is adversely affected because we do not please others, the desire for affirmation has become a need. People-pleasers are often those who feed on the attention, affirmation, and approval of others.

4. *We are unaware of our emotional limits.* We all have limits, whether they are physical, fiscal, emotional, social, spatial, or chronological. When we are out of touch with our boundaries and we pursue the making-others-happy idea, we tend to go beyond our capacity. We become emotionally overdrawn. The repetitious cycle goes like this: See a need (they're all around us); try to fix the need and make the person happy; you find this more difficult than perceived so you work harder to solve the problem; you see other needs and try to respond to them; you experience less than satisfying results, which frustrates you; you overextend your time and resources and begin to feel taken advantage of; you are near burnout so you pull back to recuperate; you renew yourself and see a need . . . and the cycle repeats itself. Healthy people understand they cannot be all things to all people all the time. If they get stuck in the people-pleasing mode, they will ultimately be no good to anyone.

Becoming Your Own Best Ally

Play to an Audience of One

There is only one person in your audience whom you need to please, your Creator. When you're bent on pleasing others, you make them out to be gods and you'll be frustrated trying to make the gods happy. Much has been written in recent years about co-dependency. The layman's definition is when one person gains personal satisfaction from aiding the dysfunction of another. Attached to many drug users or alcoholics are co-dependent people, those who stick with the individual but who are unwilling to risk strong confrontation of the destructive behavior. The co-dependent person has taken the people-pleasing behavitude to a lower level.

I mention the idea of co-dependency here because many of us may be more aware of this well-publicized dysfunction than we are of the idea of people-pleasing. The co-dependent mind-set is not far removed from its people-pleasing cousin. To tie your self-image to another person's approval or acceptance is self-defeating.

Recognize People-Pleasing Behavior

Awareness is key to overcoming nearly all of the behavitudes in this book. Usually blind to the characteristics of behavitudes, we justify our attitudes and actions to perpetuate them, rather than searching out the reasons for them. Look in yourself for the symptoms of people-pleasing. Do you find yourself trying to get the attention of others or always talking about yourself or working long and hard to make someone else happy? Do you feel taken advantage of because others' responses are not what you wanted? Do you compromise your own values at times to feel accepted? Do you feel guilty afterward, knowing you cheated your conscience? Do you feel sad and even rejected when certain individuals are distant and aloof? Do you feel frustrated unless you are able to cheer up certain people and put them in a good mood?

Establish Your Self-Worth

After you have recognized in yourself people-pleasing behavior, work hard to mentally adopt the image of God loving you unconditionally. Put your faith in him. Let his arms surround you, so that no positive or negative response from others can cause you to question your inherent value. Your value comes from being created in the image of God, not your own self-acquired means. Remind yourself over and over of this image, especially when you come into contact with people whom you have tried to please in the past. When one of these people fails to give you the recognition you feel you want or deserve, return to the image of God's love for you. One of my favorite health statements is: *What you think of me is none of my business.* We worry far too often about what others are thinking of us, allowing our perceptions of their opinions to dictate our well-being.

Give Tough Love

Finally, seek specific situations when you can show people tough love, constructively confronting a dysfunction or string-pulling behavior. String-pullers often surround themselves with people-pleasers because they are easy to manipulate. When you stand up to an injustice committed by a person whose approval you desire, you run the risk of losing that affirmation. But this is a step toward your own recovery from the people-pleasing cycle. Ironically, healthy people will respect you for this demonstration of strength, while unhealthy people will try harder to manipulate you, withholding approval or dangling carrots of applause in front of you. They are apt to reject you until they are able to work through their own insecurities. Sometimes when you try to break the people-pleasing cycle, things will get worse before they get better.

People-pleasers are often rescuers, willing to sacrifice whatever it takes to hold things together and make others happy. Whether it is taking too much responsibility to help squabbling adult siblings resolve a conflict or spending inordinate energy trying to meet your friends' expectations or resenting your demanding boss at the end of the day because of your paranoia about making him or her happy, soft love rarely provides long-term benefit to the giver or receiver. The best love is to encourage people to become their own rescuers by helping them turn to the Creator for help and satisfaction.

SELF-SABOTAGE ASSESSMENT

Place a value of 1 to 5 in the box beside each statement: 1 = no/rarely 2 = infrequently 3 = sometimes 4 = usually 5 = yes/always

☐ 1. I can stand up for myself when I feel I'm being taken advantage of.

☐ 2. I am able to say no to people without lingering guilt, when I feel their invitation will cause me to compromise on something important.

☐ 3. I ask for help when I need it.

☐ 4. Others are seldom able to take advantage of me.

☐ 5. I easily maintain my positive attitude regardless of those around me.

Add the numbers and divide by 5. If your score is 1–2.5, you are probably being an enemy to yourself in this area. If your score is 2.6–3.75, you may want to consider this area more to see what is fuzzy or what

you could do to improve it. If your score is over 3.75, you are either strong in this area or partially blind, which may require a perspective of someone who knows you well.

Self-sabotage assessment: _____

Another person's assessment of me: _____

UNPACKING PROCEDURES

1. Think of a person who appears to have a people-pleasing problem. What are the symptoms that indicate this to you?
2. Think of someone you admire who is able to lovingly say no or confront injustice without unhealthy concern for pleasing others. Why do you think this person is able to do this?
3. Think of a time when you tried to win the applause and approval of another person and it backfired so that you felt bad about it later. How would you do it differently next time?
4. How can you become a people-server without becoming a people-pleaser? Illustrate with an example if you can.
5. What is keeping you from basing your self-image on your God-given worth?
6. What is something you can do today that will demonstrate your desire to love others regardless of their response to you?

Eleven

STONE-THROWING, GNAT-STRAINING, CAMEL-SWALLOWING, SPECK-PICKING, PLANK-AVOIDING BEHAVITUDES

It's a Friday night social after work. People mingle over drinks and snacks. Suddenly you find yourself in a familiar situation. People are talking about someone else in the office.

"Bill is such an ogre. He has no idea what we do all day, and then he expects us to interrupt our projects to respond to his whims and demands," an administrative assistant says.

"I can imagine," a peer of Bill's suggests. "I was in a meeting with him last week and he had nothing good to say about the support staff of this office. The guy seems to be impossible to please."

"I heard that his marriage is on the rocks too," a woman chimes in. "He's probably a bear to live with. I hope his wife takes him to the cleaners."

Then someone turns to you, "What do you think about Bill?" she asks.

The eyes of the group are on you. What do you do? Do you toss your couple of logs on the Bill-fire? You have a couple within reach. Do you try to defend Bill, to give the verbal lynch mob a different perspective? Or do you graciously excuse yourself and avoid these people the rest of the evening? If you're like most, you'll stay and serve as an unofficial prosecutor in the trial of Bill and indulge in the self-defeating behavitude of stone-throwing.

Description and Dangers

Woe to you, teachers of the law and Pharisees, you hypocrites! You give a tenth of your spices—mint, dill and cummin. But you have neglected the more important matters of the law—justice, mercy and faithfulness. You should have practiced the latter, without neglecting the former. You blind guides! You strain out a gnat but swallow a camel.

Matthew 23:23–24

How can you say to your brother, "Brother, let me take the speck out of your eye," when you yourself fail to see the plank in your own eye? You hypocrite, first take the plank out of your eye, and then you will see clearly to remove the speck from your brother's eye.

Luke 6:42

When they kept on questioning [Jesus], he straightened up and said to them, "If any one of you is without sin, let him be the first to throw a stone at her."

John 8:7

Our tendency to point out the weaknesses of others is a way to avoid facing our own shortcomings and areas needing improvement. Stone-throwing and speck-picking behaviors include:

- Cutting down another person who is not able to defend himself or herself
- Verbalizing constructive suggestions for another person when that person is not present
- Saying something about someone in a way that you would not want the other person to hear
- Seething quietly about the weaknesses of another person
- Persistent irritability about petty behaviors or characteristics of another person
- Strategizing and even carrying out ways to sabotage another person's reputation or work or to demotivate him or her
- Expressing a critical, condemning attitude about individuals in certain roles (for example, taxicab drivers, CEOs, secretaries), classes, or races
- Making negative comments about another person as a "concern" or a "prayer request."

When is stone-throwing different from legitimate concern? Let me attempt to differentiate between what is healthy and unhealthy. Unhealthy stone-throwing exists when:

No meaningful dialogue exists. Too many "constructive critiques" are either monologue in nature, or they are dialogues in the subject's absence. By disallowing honest feedback from the person we're critiquing, we limit our ability to gather the truth and discern the wisest response. Meaningful dialogue occurs when the person being discussed is present, so that any corrections of behavior or attitude can be set in motion. Unfortunately, when the other person is present, we usually avoid talking about our concerns because we don't want to be held responsible for what we say. Perhaps we also do not really want to know the facts because we enjoy the dark side of talking about others.

Confrontation includes punishment. Even if it is your job to carry out judgment as a boss, parent, or superior, entering into the confrontation, rock in hand, almost always reflects close-minded communication. I live in Arizona where a bit of the old West remains. Public buildings have signs that say, "No deadly weapons allowed." We need to check our guns, stones, and punishments at the door before we try to enter into positive confrontation.

The accuser takes no blame or stake in the solution. Guilty parties need to own responsibility for their actions. But healthy prosecutors must bear the burden in part for the conditions that helped create the problem or at least share responsibility in finding an effective, proactive solution. Whenever we are responsible for carrying out justice, we also need to be held accountable for helping retool the conditions to avoid future irresponsibility. Considering this, we are less likely to jump into condemning others because we bear the heavier load of helping fix the problem, not just wielding the hammer.

Another's failure does not provoke our humility and sense of frailty. The delusion of self-righteousness is hidden behind the facade of condemnation. The temptation to consider ourselves worthy and above reproach is one of the negative side effects of finger pointing. Every time we pick at the speck in another's eye, we run the risk of becoming blind to our own faults. People who want to avoid self-defeating behaviors understand this risk and therefore do not frequent this behavitude.

Do you have the following symptoms of the stone-throwing behavitude?

1. You tend to be critical of the actions, motives, or attitudes of others.
2. You treat people differently in their presence than in their absence.
3. You rarely share personal failures or weaknesses or admit to wrongs when you commit them.

The Danger of Self-Righteousness

Stone-throwing makes us feel better than we really are, creating in us the idea that we're above others, giving us a false sense of security and a justification for our pride. We're like Charlie the Tuna in the old Star Kist tuna commercials. He was always trying to impress Star Kist with his good taste, but it was all superficial—he didn't taste good. By pointing out the errors of others, we strive to elevate ourselves above them. The psychological advantage of being better than others is a cheap way of bolstering a lousy self-image. Unfortunately, marring someone else's furniture is no way to make ours look any better. Pride is little more than pseudo–self-esteem, a fake copy of the real thing. When we are self-righteous, we delude ourselves into believing that we're okay because others are *not* okay. This is hardly a logical or healthy line of thought.

The Danger of Avoiding Our Own Problems

Do you ever wonder why the tabloids, sleazy talk shows, and television news magazines are so popular? When people are preoccupied with other people's dirt, they don't have time to worry about cleaning up their own. Their preoccupation can even serve to justify their avoidance of their own messes.

This placebo effect does not get us very far, but the temporary painkiller is enough to keep a lot of us bent on fixing the world before we fix ourselves. Just as a magician performs sleight of hand by misdirecting our attention, we "magically" make our weaknesses and sins disappear by focusing attention on others instead of on ourselves. For a short time we may avert responsibility for our own faults, but we end up sabotaging our potential for growth.

The Danger of Alienating Others

Behind the biblical story of the woman caught in adultery was more than likely a warm, hurting, well-intentioned though misdirected woman. By stone-casting, the human judges were not taking the time and effort to understand this woman. Their jump to conclusion probably prevented them from knowing her past, her motives, or even hearing her side of the story. Stone-throwing is easier than understanding and getting to the root of the problem.

Because so much stone-throwing takes place among "friends" and associates, we create all sorts of awkward situations. We have to act nice around the people we've assassinated in the lunch room. At family reunions we have to pretend everything's okay, when in reality we're at odds with some of our relatives. We feel guilty and dishonest for saying one thing and doing another. This game-playing and hypocritical behavior detracts from our self-esteem and destroys the hopes for a significant friendship with the person whom we've "stoned." The victim may never know why we don't become a friend, but *we* do. Indulging in stone-throwing can leave us alienated and alone, without the love and acceptance we desire.

The Danger of Becoming Known for Stone-Throwing

If you talk to me about others behind their back, what will you do behind *my* back? Unfortunately stone-throwers have few intimate friends because what goes around comes around. The paranoia that develops after tossing a few rocks at others is enough to make us all defensive. Stone-throwers are not fully honest and open. They rarely experience intimacy, which is a by-product of being loved and accepted as we are, warts and all. While there is often a herd effect to stone-throwing and gossips usually travel in groups, these social circles are often superficial. Who wants a friend who talks about you behind your back? How do I know I can trust you to say good things in my absence when I've seen you cut up a "friend" behind his or her back, only to smile and act endearing when the person unexpectedly appears?

The Impetus behind Stone-Throwing

Why do we so often indulge in finding fault with others and talking about them behind their back? Here are four reasons:

1. *We are familiar with our own failures and recognize them in others.* Psychologists call this transference. We transfer to others what we see in ourselves. When you buy a certain color and model of vehicle, you suddenly become aware of similar models and colors on the road. Your eye grows familiar with the one you own. It's the same principle at work when you see your weaknesses in others.

   Pointing out the faults of others, keeping the attention on them, conveys the idea that we have our act together. We pretend to be a certified expert on human behavior and therefore qualified to critique others. By setting up smoke screens and pointing to other people's real or perceived errors, we keep the crowd from staring at our imperfections.

2. *Peer pressure.* The desire to be accepted and to fit in is never more evident than when we chime in on a verbal lynching. Psychologists have studied the effects of mob psychology for years. They know that good, well-meaning people can do some pretty outlandish things, just because of peer pressure.

When we drop our guard and join others tossing rocks, we feel an immediate sense of gratification that comes with belonging and winning the approval of the group, but the euphoria is temporary. Undermining the intentions and character of others damages us as much as the person we're stoning. When other stone-throwers talk us into mugging someone else, it reveals our own lack of self-identity and willpower. Conscious or subconscious shame results. Long-term guilt and remorse will follow and may defeat us. Dipping our hands into manure is sure to leave an odorous residue. We can't smell like roses when we're slopping the hogs.

3. *We have seen stone-throwing modeled all our lives.* We learn by watching, listening, and experiencing significant others in our lives. Unfortunately, because stone-throwing is so common, we've grown up believing this is a normal and therefore healthy behavitude. We toss stones at the waitress, the new office policy, the pastor's Sunday message, the neighbor's yard work, and TV sports. The list is practically endless. In fact we do it so often that most of us are blind to this behavitude; the habit has become second nature in our conversations and daily life.

4. *Regarding faults, our natural perspective looks outward, not inward.* Have you ever noticed that it's easier to spot the lingering piece of spinach in the teeth of

your dinner guest than it is in your own teeth? Not until you look in a mirror or whisper to your spouse "How're my teeth?" are you sure that your smile is food free. Anyone who hikes knows that the vista from the bottom of a mountain trail is significantly different from the view halfway up or at the top. Looking from behind our eyes, our focus is more outward than inward. We are much better able to evaluate someone else's behavior than we are our own.

Becoming Your Own Best Ally

Look for Stone-Throwing in Yourself

When you are sitting around a lunch table with work associates, begin noticing what others are saying that is less than positive about friends and associates. You probably won't have to wait long before you begin to hear it. Verbal guerrilla warfare also abounds at watercoolers, over the Internet, and on the telephone. Noticing such critical conversation is beneficial only as it reveals the kind of person who casts stones. Learn to see this behavior in others so you will recognize it in yourself.

Stick Up for the Attacked Person

When it seems appropriate, stick up for the person who is being accused or stoned. Then people will know that it's safe to be honest and real around you, and it will hold accusers accountable. If people label you as naive or a Goody Two-shoes, so be it.

So what do you do when you see someone else's fault? Do you turn your back on what you know to be right? If you don't cast a stone or two, who will notice *your* impeccable credentials and fine taste? People will think you are a characterless wimp.

When the religious zealots brought the adulterous woman to Jesus, he handled the situation well. After the accusers left, he did not say, "Whew, that was close. I guess I got you out of that one. Okay, you're out of danger. Go and remember to have safe sex from now on." Rather, his response was "I don't accuse you either; go and sin no more." In other words, you can be aware of improper attitudes, behaviors, and actions of others, without accusing them and casting stones. Refusing to throw stones is not the same as compromising on what is right. Jesus wisely moved the solution from an external one (stoning by others) to an internal one (you go and sin no more). By sticking up for the target, you hold others more accountable for what they say and provide a better perspective than one-way accusations allow.

Question Your Motives

Ask yourself the question when you are tempted to pick up a stone, *Why do I take pleasure or feel the need to do this? What am I running away from or trying to avoid in my own life? Am I guilty of some of these same issues? What good will this do me and those who listen?* We fool ourselves into thinking that we can significantly change our lives by changing other people's behavior. Certainly there is the need at times to communicate our unwillingness to participate in someone's self-destructive actions, but our first responsibility is to recognize our own sins and our Creator's view of them. When you see things in others that need correcting and that rile up your indignation, the first place to look is yourself. Let that urge to toss a rock or pick a speck cause you to look within and ask, *What do I need to work on myself? Where have I failed in the past? What have I learned from these shortcomings?*

Create Positive Influences

Some might suggest that venting frustrations is therapeutic, but nearly all stone-throwing is more like tossing a log on the fire than it is using a fire extinguisher. People who complain about the sex and violence on their VCRs are hypocrites. Similarly people who criticize others for their lack of sensitivity and their unloving behavior without the person present are doing little more than rewinding the tape on their VCR so they can replay the hurt and crime one more time. Surround yourself with people who are positive and who guard against negative talk. Distance yourself from those who indulge in stonings, verbal or otherwise. Weak people thrive on such a feeding frenzy. Strong people avoid it because of its self-defeating results. Silently walk away. Mob psychology is powerful. Getting swept away by the temptation to toss a few verbal stones is easy. "Do not let any unwholesome talk come out of your mouths, but only what is helpful for building others up according to their needs, that it may benefit those who listen" (Eph. 4:29).

SELF-SABOTAGE ASSESSMENT

Place a value of 1 to 5 in the box beside each statement: 1 = no/rarely 2 = infrequently 3 = sometimes 4 = usually 5 = yes/always

☐ 1. I stick to positive comments when talking about another person.
☐ 2. I defend people who are being maligned in their absence.

☐ 3. I refrain from jumping in or agreeing with people when they begin talking negatively about another person.

☐ 4. I consciously strive to remember my weaknesses and failures before I comment about those of other people.

☐ 5. I focus on the strengths and good points of other people instead of their flaws.

Add the numbers and divide by 5. If your score is 1–2.5, you are probably being an enemy to yourself in this area. If your score is 2.6–3.75, you may want to consider this area more to see what is fuzzy or what you could do to improve it. If your score is over 3.75, you are either strong in this area or partially blind, which may require a perspective of someone who knows you well.

Self-sabotage assessment: _____

Another person's assessment of me: _____

UNPACKING PROCEDURES

1. Why do you think people tend to be negative in their comments about other people?
2. Think of a person who commonly makes derogatory comments about other people. What does his or her criticism tell you about this individual?
3. How could you focus on the good and verbalize only what is constructive about others?

4. What can you do to turn around negative conversations without making people feel overly guilty?
5. How can your critical attitude about others reveal that you have blind spots when you look at yourself?
6. Think of a person who verbalizes only what is positive about others. What can you learn from this constructive behavior?
7. How can you come across as positive without appearing naive, mediocre, or approving of a person whose attitudes or behaviors are not commendable?

Twelve

RUN AND HIDE

Our business was failing. I didn't know why we weren't making a profit. I was working day and night, giving up sleep, compromising on my family time. I couldn't figure it out. But instead of asking for help from my more successful friends or contacts, I never told a soul. When someone asked, "How's business?" I'd respond, "It's going great." Sure it was. We had to lay off our employees and eventually file for bankruptcy. As I look back, I'm so embarrassed I didn't ask for help. I dismissed the few suggestions I got from friends, figuring I could solve the problems myself. I realize they were trying to show me things that I had overlooked, but I saw it as prying into my business. I was so stinking proud, I did not see reality. My marriage suffered as a result. We nearly got a divorce.

Description and Dangers

Truth can be very intimidating. Discovering certain things about ourselves or others is painful at times. It may be a personal blind spot or flaw, bad news about health, or a dismal business projection. Sometimes the saying seems true: Ignorance is bliss. If we're about to be mugged or pursued by an enemy, our natural response is to either run or hide. When we perceive truth as an enemy and run and hide from it, we defeat ourselves and avoid what will ultimately help us.

Do you have the following symptoms of running and hiding from truth?

1. You avoid accountability relationships and intimacy where truth is often told.
2. You ignore feedback from others that addresses weaknesses or areas needing improvement.
3. You deny problems when they are pointed out, either by blaming other people, ending communication, or walking away from the situation.

The Danger of Missing the Opportunity to Become a Better Person

A woodworker puts his plane, file, and sandpaper to use in crafting a beautiful piece of furniture. When the tool comes in contact with the lumber, there is friction, but eventually the friction produces beauty. In our lives, facing truth can cause friction. It may force us to think or act differently, which can be difficult for us, so we tend to avoid any truth that would make us change. We'd rather stay the way we are. We exchange short-term peace for long-term benefit. With enough compromise of the truth, we end up with disappointment and lost opportunity.

The Bible says that people enjoy darkness because of their evil deeds. I've discovered that what bothers me most about the Bible is not what I don't understand, but what I do. If I don't want to grow spiritually or in character, I avoid prayer, reading the Bible, or close accountability with people who do. Perhaps this is the primary reason we avoid quiet time with God, because we're fearful of what we may need to change.

The Danger of a Habit

Truth avoidance is an avocation for many. Like playing dodgeball in the schoolyard, we run from being hit, sometimes hiding behind someone else. We somehow think that truth is our enemy instead of our ally, that it'll take us out of the game instead of helping us win. Occasionally, very occasionally, truth does complicate matters. Confessing to a crime can send us to jail. Telling someone that you've gossiped about him or her can put the relationship on ice. Admitting to an affair may end the marriage. There are times when telling the truth is best done between us and our Creator. Honesty is the best policy always. But openness is not always the prudent thing. Honesty and openness are related but different issues. We must be sensitive about how and why we express honesty. As a general rule, embracing truth provides long-term benefit. When we neglect the truth, there will be a twinge of pain in our conscience, but enduring that twinge once, then twice, easily becomes habit-forming.

The Danger of Alienating People

Because people are often truth vehicles, when we run from the truth we run from our relationships. We see someone we do not want to confront, so we avoid him or her at the office, go down a different aisle at the grocery store, and pick a different workout time so we don't have to interact with the person at the gym. We've all experienced the tension that exists when we're out of sync with a friend or family member. We need people if we are to be whole and well-adjusted. By running from the truth, we interrupt relationships and have to shop for more.

For example, let's say that your spouse wants to talk very honestly about how you've been treating her. You've been unconsciously allowing the stress at work to affect your communication. When you come home, you're irritable, short-tempered, and quiet. When she welcomes you and asks how the day was, you mumble at her and tell her to "forget it." Your responses have wilted her, so that she's feeling alienated and sad.

She tries to tell you how she feels about your behavior, but you have various ways you can run and hide. You can avoid her by putting in long hours at work and being "too tired" to talk when you do get home. You can try to pacify her frustrations by quickly admitting guilt and giving an "I'll try better" response in hopes of getting her off your back as soon as possible. You can intimidate her with physical force, thus shutting up the source of truth-telling. You can give her the cold treatment, punishing her emotionally for raising a concern. Or you can go into a defensive mode, which implies she's "out of her gourd" and doesn't understand what you're going through.

Because truth is avoided by either stifling it or running from it, the situation only worsens. Soon the bed is cold as you turn your backs to each other at night. Meals are quiet times of eye wandering and shallow discussion about mundane matters. You're miserable. She's miserable.

You have the ability to make things better, but you don't, because to do that would require facing the truth about your lack of communication. So what you vowed would never happen occurs—you've become like your parents. You're like the older couples you've noticed at restaurants. They sit through a whole meal without talking. After avoiding the truth so many times, a callus grows over your emotions. You don't feel love anymore. You and your wife linger in marriage, enduring each other. There are long periods of silence broken occasionally by friendly laughter, small remnants of yesteryear's affection. It doesn't need to be this way, but running and hiding from truth has its consequences. Intimate relationships can become shallow when we're afraid to confront reality. Some of us give up on replenishing the relationships we've ruined and we become hermits, lonely people in the midst of crowds.

The Danger of Making the Problem Worse

Procrastination is a form of running from the truth in that you avoid confronting an issue. While you're mustering the courage to see the doctor, the cancer can be spreading to the point of no return. The tooth that pained you earlier has become infected. The ear infection that went unchecked turns into a raging fever. The knock under the hood ruins the engine.

Dealing with truth is a daily responsibility. If you run from the truth for long, small problems can become giant catastrophes. Hurricanes and earthquakes attract our attention, but termites cause more damage annually than both of these disasters combined. Tiny bites can save us or ruin us because most problems tend to get bigger with inattention but working at them little by little can solve them. Only a small minority of problems go away if we ignore them.

Avoiding Truth

Why do we run and hide from the truth when doing so can be our ruin? Here are four reasons:

1. *We're too busy.* Busyness is often a smoke screen for a messy inner life. When we fail to live within our margins, we get overwhelmed when someone needs to talk or we need to stop and deal with the matters at hand. Confronting, unloading, and figuring out what we're going to do with the truth when we face it take time, and, depending on the kind of truth, the process usually requires us to emotionally disengage for a period as well.

Generally, when the need to deal with truth confronts us, we have not planned for it, but we must make room for it. When we're overcommitted or unwilling to prioritize the time, we toss the truth on the counter like an unopened utility bill. Not opening it does not mean it's paid, that we'll have enough money in the bank to cover it, or that our electricity won't get turned off as a result. In the same way, the need to confront the truth won't just go away.

2. *We know we're not where we need to be, so outta sight, outta mind.* Little kids love the game of peekaboo. Cover your face with your hands or merely close your eyes. Open them up, say "boo" and they giggle in response. The funny thing about little kids is that when they close their eyes, they actually think you disappear. They think, *What I don't see doesn't exist.*

Unfortunately peekaboo is a mind game for many adults. They think that as long as they avoid a problem, it goes away. Many people avoid spiritual truths by simply staying away from church. They say things such as, "Church is irrelevant, boring, stiff, and dull." Granted, many churches are, but if people really confronted their need for moral, spiritual, and inner strength, they would do what it takes to find a congregation that is alive and healthy.

Deceiving ourselves, we think we can hide, and the truth and/or its consequences won't find us. Basically we're afraid and we close our eyes to the unknown. We'd rather deal with the known because it has become familiar and comfortable, even though it may be unfulfilling and even unhappy. By turning our backs on our looming problems, we create a virtual reality where these threats do not exist.

3. *We don't like pain.* No one likes pain, but it comes in all sizes, shapes, and forms to all of us. Sometimes the pain produces something extremely good. When

we embrace that young infant after a difficult delivery, we know the pain was worth it. When we see that we got straight As, we're glad we put in the long hours of study. When we first face truth, though, we don't know what the outcome will be, so we're tempted to avoid the pain the truth may bring and run or hide.

Truth about ourselves often makes us look imperfect, revealing our faults and failures. Even though we may believe that the long-term benefits of criticism or discipline will be positive, we never enjoy experiencing them. But when our self-esteem is based on the idea of perfection, as opposed to our innate value, we cosmetically cover the blemishes and avoid situations that might mess up our makeup. My wife is an incredibly loving woman, not to mention beautiful, even though this next illustration may not give that appearance. After she has applied a fresh coat of lipstick, we'll start to kiss hello or goodbye and she'll say, "I have lipstick," meaning "If you kiss me right now, it will smear my lips." So I either kiss her cheek or we air kiss. While she saved her looks, she lost a good kiss. The word picture is that preserving our image often keeps us from kissing the truth.

4. *As creatures of habit, we don't want to change.* Confronting the truth often requires us to do something different, which means adding or deleting a behavior. Doing something different often means we must move from our comfort zones. A strange thing about humans is that we're prone to like our habits, even bad ones. I often walked through the fields of our family farm on paths created by the cattle traveling to and from water holes and feeding areas. Even though these dirt trails were not the shortest or

fastest way from point A to B, I took them because they were well worn.

We like our well-worn paths in life. Facing truth usually requires some sort of change, whether miniscule or significant, some movement off the path. Change is an interesting thing. Even though we need it to grow and to survive in an ever-evolving world, we often avoid it. Change is usually preceded by truth, some sort of insight that either creates excitement for the future or is a painful reality check about what's not going well.

Becoming Your Own Best Ally

Seek Input and Accountability

When you get used to personal growth and observation, you tend to stay more flexible and less brittle. Looking at life as a fluid state helps us develop a disposition where truth can find a home. Like raking the soil prepares a garden to receive a seed, the introspective life welcomes truth and even pursues it. Reading books, listening to new ideas, pondering feedback from people, and asking questions are all vehicles for introspection.

Most people talk too much and listen too little. It is difficult to introspect well when you're talking, unless you are probing deeper into an issue. Introspection considers feelings, facts, circumstances, feedback, and discrepancies between what you say and do. You become your own worst enemy when you avoid truth and don't seek it. The beauty of asking for ideas and feedback is threefold.

1. It allows you to proactively seek truth, thus putting you in more of a controlled position versus a defensive, reactive role. When others confront you with

possible truth, sometimes it is incongruent with your emotional state, thus diminishing your ability or willingness to respond with an open mind. Sometimes you reject truth because you are caught on the defensive emotionally. Like a knee-jerk reaction, you turn off the person or idea because it catches you off guard. The natural response when cornered is to fight back. But by taking the initiative, you set the pace in seeking truth from others, or at least their perspectives. You get to select the time, context, and even the moods of other people when you will ask for truth.

2. Seeking truth from others keeps you familiar with hearing and processing reality. Rarely do you find a pure gold nugget of truth. You usually have to refine the opinions, feedback, and ideas from others. But even an off-base criticism may have a hint of truth and can lead to a better grasp of reality. Just as an athlete must stretch out to stay flexible, asking for input helps us avoid stiff emotional joints. Just as eating properly and exercising can keep your arteries unclogged, keeping truth flowing avoids hardening of the attitudes.

3. Seeking truthful input on a regular basis diminishes the need for large truth dumping. Because of busyness or just the emotional hassles that dealing with difficult issues can create, we tend to store them up to be dealt with later. Keeping up with truth issues, however, helps us avoid a sudden barrage of stored-up problems. There is a time for spring cleaning, but daily and weekly upkeep helps us avoid huge cleanups all at once. Annual job reviews are fine, but regular discussions about behaviors, problems, and potential obstacles allow an office atmosphere to be clear of the overhanging gloom that truth avoidance creates. Wiping the slate clean on a frequent basis is

what truth seeking is about. If people are not honest with you, shame on them. If you are not asking for input, you are opening yourself up for dumping episodes, which no one enjoys.

Admit Your Imperfections

Make a conscious effort to note how often you admit wrong, say "I'm sorry," humbly accept blame without pointing fingers, or ask for help. Better yet, ask those who know you well but who do not stand to lose anything by being honest if you seem to be aware of and admit your own imperfections. Pride is a natural filter that sifts out truth that may be detrimental to our ego. Putting yourself down is different from admitting what everyone already knows. The beauty of admitting failures is that when you beat someone who may want to point them out, you take the wind out of their sails. Friends appreciate humility.

Understand God's Acceptance

God's acceptance of you is not the same as approval of your failures. You can accept a person without approving his attitudes, actions, or motivations. Many well-meaning people who call themselves Christians reject other people because they disapprove of something about them. Jesus modeled the sort of conservative values and liberal grace that drives many people nuts when they try to figure it out. Regardless, God's acceptance is a solution to the fear we feel when we want to face a truth but run and hide instead. As kids, we played hide-and-seek. When time was up and everyone had not been caught or made it home, the "it" person would yell, "Allie, allie in free." The really good hiders could then walk in without the threat of being caught.

God is yelling, "Allie, allie in free." He paid your ticket. He bought your freedom. It's on him, free, but not cheap. Hide no more, surrender. The consequence is acceptance! Come home!

Learn How to Tell Truth Well

We can't close a look at truth avoidance without turning our gaze on the way we tell the truth to others. All of us can remember at least one time when someone told us the truth about ourselves so poorly that we are forever marked by the negative experience. Even though we know the pain that improper truth-telling brings, we often do the same to others. We are our own worst enemy when we mishandle confronting others because botched truth-telling jobs can end viable relationships. While we cannot take responsibility for other people's reactions, we can own up to partial blame when we present truth insensitively, negatively, and with scorn. Here are some guiding principles to help you offer truth to others.

Have I earned the right? What gives you the right or responsibility to confront this person? Do you know his or her circumstances well enough? Armchair critics are a dime a dozen. What makes you an authority on this truth you want to share?

If you have indeed earned the right, then don't just sit there in silence as your friend suffers from a lack of truth. "Wounds from a friend can be trusted, but an enemy multiplies kisses" (Prov. 27:6). Friends don't let friends lack truth. "Ya, I didn't think he was the right man for you all along," a girlfriend admits after the breakup. "So when were you going to tell me this—after my honeymoon?"

On one side, we've got people who love us, unwilling to confront us with truth, and on the other side we have total strangers who feel free to tell it the way they see it.

Drive-by truth-tellings for the most part are acts of irresponsibility that have the potential of alienating us from others.

Do it at the right time, yours and theirs. Stupid—that's what some people are in the way they confront. They don't consider the factors that will make the truth-telling more palatable to the listener: the person's mood, the proper timing, the context. Truth-telling is perhaps more a matter of how than what. Truth is not going to find a happy home when you present it irresponsibly. Often people don't reject the truth but react to how it was delivered. It's akin to tossing your girlfriend an engagement ring and saying, "Hey, if you wanna marry me, put it on." That's why engagement rings come in classy velvet boxes. In a "presentation is everything" world, we have a lot to learn about how we deliver truth.

You also need to know when it is right for you to share the truth. When you or the other person is mad, overly emotional, tired, hungry, or stressed, neither of you will be able to be objective. Sometimes, the truth-telling can't wait, but quite often, you can find a time that is good for you and for the other person so that you can communicate the truth well and your listener can receive it. If your motive is to help instead of hurt, you'll pay as much attention to when and how as to what.

Get the facts. Irresponsible truth-tellers don't know the facts. They jump to conclusions, based on hearsay and second-, third-, and fourth-party feedback. They fill in the blanks and assume underlying motives.

Inner motivations are very difficult to ascertain. If you have sufficient evidence to confront, assume an "I may be wrong" initial position. Certainly if it is a matter of sharing your feelings, you can do this, but contextualize it as being your perception as opposed to a hard, cold fact. Too many times, our final opinion is quite different from our initial one, so we avoid defeating ourselves by leaving room for new evidence as the case is presented. "Did you mean this when you said this?" "Help me understand why you . . ."

Go to the source of the problem. The world is full of great big sissies, people who would rather conduct guerrilla warfare behind someone's back than go to the person and deal with the issue. Gossip and innuendo are their ammunition. People who refuse to go to the source of their problems are communicating a lack of character, a presence of fear, and an inability to solve issues. If you are in this position, stop your whimpering about other people to other people. Victim talk is debilitating and self-debasing. Besides, it tends to discourage those who hear but can do nothing to resolve the situation. Go to the person who has offended you and communicate.

Sometimes we avoid confronting a person because we don't want resolution; we want a reason to bellyache. This is self-defeating. The "woe is me" and "I've been done wrong" songs are endless. Recognize the rut you're in because of your complaining and resolve to put an end to it by going to the person and telling him or her the truth with sensitivity and gentleness. And then enjoy life *without* complaining about what someone else has done to you.

Make suggestions, not demands. Focus on the future, not the past. What can we do to fix the issue, not just mull over the problem? Pleading for help is far more productive than commanding it be done "my way or the highway." Let me say again that success in truth-telling is in the how far more than in the what.

The congregation I pastor is part of a genre of churches that strives to engage people who have been turned off by churches in the past. We have a large number of people (60–70 percent) who either have no church background or had given up on traditional church prior to attending.

Other churches often criticize congregations like ours because they think we dilute the Bible by making it applicable and understandable. The biggest difference is in our presentation. You can say the same things and be either offensive or endearing. What most people find objectionable about Christian people is not the truth they tell as much as how they tell it. They confuse form with essence, assuming people are rejecting the essence of their message instead of its form. Apparently it never dawns on them that their communication challenge might be self-induced, that their presentation is offensive, and people are rejecting them, not their message. Often people cannot even hear our truth because the attitude or style of our truth-telling gets in the way. By making suggestions or asking for help, you're more likely to find a home for truth in the other person. Homeless truth does no one any good.

Follow-Up. After truth-telling, when it is feasible, follow-up is vital. Too much mulling goes on after truth-telling takes place that can distort both thoughts and emotions. I have found it very important, a day or so after a confrontation, to ask the other person, "Are we okay? Is there anything else that has come to mind that might help us? How are things?" Far too often, in the midst of truth-telling, we get caught up in the process. Afterward, we have other ideas, think of things we might have said, or have a lingering bad taste. You do not have to rewind the truth-telling episode, but following up gives you an idea of how the other person received what you said and if there's anything else that needs to be addressed. You will be able to tell if the other person is still ticked off or if he or she seems to be fine. When we do not take care of adequate follow-up, we often have to go back and handle other issues related to our truth-telling. Follow-up conveys the idea that the relationship and the person are important to you.

SELF-SABOTAGE ASSESSMENT

Place a value of 1 to 5 in the box beside each statement: 1 = no/rarely 2 = infrequently 3 = sometimes 4 = usually 5 = yes/always

- [ ] 1. I am open to people telling me ways I can improve.
- [ ] 2. I go to the source of the problem when I am offended or bothered by something someone has done or said.
- [ ] 3. I seek advice from others as to how I can improve or do better.
- [ ] 4. I am open to ideas that will help me improve my life and/or show me where I may be erring.
- [ ] 5. I humbly admit I am wrong and/or that I have weaknesses.

Add the numbers and divide by 5. If your score is 1–2.5, you are probably being an enemy to yourself in this area. If your score is 2.6–3.75, you may want to consider this area more to see what is fuzzy or what you could do to improve it. If your score is over 3.75, you are either strong in this area or partially blind, which may require a perspective of someone who knows you well.

Self-sabotage assessment: _____

Another person's assessment of me: _____

UNPACKING PROCEDURES

1. Think of someone you know who is humble and good at receiving criticism. How do you think he or she developed this ability?
2. Think of a time when you ran or hid from the truth. What did you learn from this situation?
3. Think of a time when you confronted the truth and/or received criticism well. What went right?
4. Think of a time when you confronted another person and it went very well. Why did it go well?
5. Think of a time when you confronted another person and it went poorly. Why did it go poorly?
6. Name two to four people who hold you accountable in various arenas of your life. What holes exist where there is very little accountability? What are the potential dangers of these holes?

Thirteen

BURIED TREASURE

I always wanted to be a flight attendant. I like people. I love to travel. I enjoy serving people. Ever since I was a child, after taking my first vacation by plane, I knew that was something I wanted to try. But my parents mocked my dream and said it would be a waste of energy for me to go to college only to do something that had such limitations. Even though I disagreed with them, they were helping me get my own apartment after high school, so I somehow felt obliged to do as they thought best.

I never completed a college degree. I never became a flight attendant. I know there is no fantasy job. I understand that the grass often appears greener in someone else's yard. But when I travel, I still have that sense that I would like to do that as a living. I got married, had kids, and certainly don't regret my time invested in them. But now that the kids are grown, I regret not having pursued my dreams.

Description and Dangers

You were born with a unique blend of talents and passions, and you are thereby granted corresponding opportunities. This is not the same idea popularized by American motivators who suggest you can be anything you want to be if you just believe. That kind of bologna has ultimately discouraged people far more than it has encouraged them. After we get over the inspiration and bump our heads a few times when trying to do things we're not gifted to do, we become disillusioned.

Carte blanche possibilities do not exist for anyone, regardless of network, talent, or drive. Everyone has time, talent, and energy limitations. No matter how much I want it, I cannot become an NBA star. Saying that we can't be whatever we want does not necessarily limit becoming what we ought to be. Corresponding with our God-given gifts and abilities are Creator-ordained callings and inner inklings of what we need to be. Because these oughts are within us, we decide whether to let them out or hold them in.

Do you have the following symptoms of keeping your treasure buried?

1. You tell "woe is me" stories to friends, lamenting what you could have been "if only."
2. You feel irritable and bitter as a result of mourning lost destiny.
3. You daydream about what your life could have been had you pursued the music within you.

The Danger of Lost Opportunities

A major danger of burying our talents is losing the corresponding opportunities to experience accomplishments and fulfillment in life. Do you remember the story that Jesus told about talents? The man who had received one talent gave his excuse. "So I was afraid and went out and hid your talent in the ground" (Matt. 25:25). While many think of the talent in the parable as an ability talent, careful analysis teaches us a different lesson. The talent represented the power and potential to *use* an ability, not the ability itself. The steward chose what to do with his talent. He could have invested it in a venture or blue chip company, put it on deposit in a bank to collect interest, or created a new business to increase the money's original value.

When we bury the gifts we have been given, we will sense lost opportunities and experience remorse, frustration, and a subtle irritability toward life in general. Jealousy toward those using their opportunities separates us from potential and existing friends. Even though we may have a large family and many friends, the alone feeling created by talent burying will turn us into emotional islands. Misery may love company, but it tends to be mutual loneliness as opposed to unified camaraderie.

The Danger of Buck Passing

A major theme of this book is how much finger pointing and buck passing go on in most self-defeating behavitudes. Jesus' parable shows us that we often blame our inaction on others. The foolish steward suggested that his decision to bury his talent was based on the owner's demanding expectations. The owner did not buy into the man's excuse, however, and confronted him about it. The steward had lost his opportunity to make a difference with what he'd been entrusted. Although we may give a plethora of reasons why we're not using our gifts and talents, the responsibility always falls back on us. Life has a way of holding us accountable.

The Danger of Lost Vitality

When we bury our dreams and talents, we lose vitality for living. Psychologist Victor Frankl, who observed first-hand the responses of people within Nazi concentration camps, and Dr. Dennis Waitley, who interviewed Vietnam POWs, teach us that even in extremely adverse conditions, those who are dream pursuers fare far better than dream buryers. When we pursue our dreams and implement our ambitions, we create the by-product hope, which everyone needs to get through the stresses of life. Without hope, people are sick more often, enjoy life less, and tend to adversely influence those around them.

"I'm just too busy and after I've finished my chores, I'm too pooped to do anything else." Usually a comment like this is a revelation that we've buried our dreams and have forgotten where. When you begin to pursue your dreams, they energize you so that you are able to find and use niches of time. This soul-fueling pursuit motivates you to reduce more of the time wasters in your daily schedule so that you are able to fulfill your yearning.

Those of us who are treasure buryers blame our frittered lives on any number of factors, but the bottom line for many of us is an inability to confront our fears. Because our gifts and destiny are so important, we greatly fear failure in their pursuit. A part of our self-image is intertwined with our dreams and callings, and we fear that failure will mar our personhood and lower our stock value. Like the foolish steward, we convince ourselves that if we don't attempt anything risky with our gifts, we won't fail. We bury our abilities for safekeeping, even though our Creator gave them to us to use.

The Danger of Regrets

I don't know how many people I've talked to who have regrets for not pursuing their dreams. Usually at midlife people begin to confront the inconsistencies between what they ought to be doing with their life and what they are doing with it. Either we accomplish enough success to help us discern the difference between success and significance, or we realize that reaching the top of our ladder is not going to get us where we want to be.

The monotony of the rat race by midlife is usually enough to jar some of us loose from our ruts. Unfortunately many of us are so encumbered by that point that our ego or bank account does not allow us the freedom to break loose and pursue our true dreams.

Not long ago I had a conversation with a man in his late thirties, which depicts an all too common story line. "I don't know what to do," he said. "I've been in the semiconductor field since my midtwenties and have done very well. Between my stock options and my wife's career, we've been able to pretty much reach all our material goals. But I don't want to do this the rest of my life. My dream is to start a nonprofit organization that would help high-risk kids adapt in society, you know, learn job skills, get mentoring, and make a life for themselves. But whenever I hint at quitting my job to do this, my wife says I'm ridiculous. She's become accustomed to a certain lifestyle and is afraid if I go out on this new venture that we'll have to give it up. We may. But I don't enjoy my work anymore. There's so much more I could be doing to make a difference in people's lives. What do I do?"

The despair and disappointment in the man's eyes are a frequent sight among people who mourn the loss of their dreams. Submerged below the surface of most of us are inner yearnings for unique significance that our heavenly Engineer has programmed into our emotional DNA.

Dream Stealers

Why do we bury our dreams when it is self-defeating? Here are four reasons:

1. *Past influencers.* Significant people in our past may have lived out their frustrations by spreading to us their bitterness and lack of faith. Because faith and

hope are fragile qualities when we are young, we are often predisposed to burying our dreams if we have been influenced in that direction by significant others. While it is primarily the responsibility of a parent to prepare a child for life and dream pursuits, in the end each of us individually must accomplish our calling. No one else can do it for us.

2. *We have not paid the price to uncover our gifts.* What is your purpose in life? Why were you born? What is it you are meant to achieve? The answer to this will invariably include and perhaps even center around your gift mix. When we are not aware of our gifts, we tend to wander.

Gifts are usually found via three avenues that work best if considered together: personal assessment, feedback from others, and experiential effectiveness. A variety of instruments is available to help us measure our gifting. Relying on others for feedback is very helpful. Do people comment positively when you use your perceived gift? Is there a desire for more of what you provide? Do they tell others about you and your gift? If we do not receive consistent, positive feedback from a variety of people when we use what we perceive as our gifts, chances are we do not really have them.

The third discovery tool is experimentation. Sometimes the only way you can know if you have a certain gift or ability is to use it. Try something that will reveal it. This often takes time. It requires energy to seek opportunities and evaluate your success in them. If you are not aware of your unique abilities, chances are you will wander through jobs, ministries, and even hobbies.

3. *Past failures.* Just as certain plants are more susceptible to adverse conditions than others, people respond differently to challenges. In our backyard, we have

beautiful but thorny bushes called bougainvillea. You can cut, slice, squish, and starve these flowery vines, but they'll come back strong. The delicate flowers in the front yard, however, are very susceptible to frost, too much sun, lack of water, or being crushed underfoot.

Depending on how you are wired, you will either thrive when challenged or crumble when you fail. I received hundreds of publisher rejection slips in my early writing years. But each note became a motivator to improve and try a different approach. The barriers honed my skills, resulting in subsequent published books and articles. Pursuing dreams is precarious in the beginning. They are like newborns—vulnerable, weak, needy, and easily injured. When we attempt new ventures and fail, we can be influenced to give up future faith attempts as well. Perhaps the loss of money, losing face in front of others, or the echoes of self-doubt encourage us to bury our talents. We confuse past failures with predictions of future success. But there is really no relationship between the two. They are different commodities.

4. *Fear of failure.* As Mark Twain wrote, we fear many things, most of which never happen. There is a direct correlation between low self-esteem and fear. People who suffer from inadequate inner love commonly struggle with attempting new ventures and taking the risk of following dreams. "There is no fear in love. But perfect love drives out fear, because fear has to do with punishment. The one who fears is not made perfect in love" (1 John 4:18). Conversely, people with high self-esteem are more confident in faith ventures and are willing to risk failure to pursue fulfillment.

God did not create us with completed dreams, only latent ones. It is our responsibility to invest in them, making them grow and turning a profit. Just as running from a bully will create a self-image of an insecure weakling, so will avoiding being beaten up by failure. This injures our self-image to the point that we lose all confidence in taking risks. There are no guarantees when it comes to fulfilling inner dreams, but you can be sure to develop regrets over buried talents.

Becoming Your Own Best Ally

Discover Your Gifts and Aptitudes

Discovering your unique gifts and aptitudes is not easy. While there is continued debate on whether talents are inbred or learned, I'm of the school that believes you are born with gift aptitudes, even if they are discovered later in life. Gifts are a part of your DNA. Most of us with children understand that basically the same home environment can yield pretty amazingly different kids. That is because we are prewired with or predisposed to certain strengths. Earlier in the chapter I mentioned three ways of uncovering your gifts. Other tools include assessments; 360-degree surveys, which collect responses from those who work below, above, and alongside you organizationally; and professional analysis. These are all helpful in showing you what you do well. Effective people don't spend a lot of energy bolstering weaknesses. Rather, they focus their attention on discovering and maximizing their strengths.

Uncover Your Passions

A talent or gift is but a tool, whereas a passion is an engine. Passion has to do with what motivates us, what makes our eyes dance with excitement. The factory worker who detests his job and grudgingly obliges his boss runs to his car after work to don a softball uniform and play ball. He loves the game. Offices are filled with people who eke out livings but long for extracurricular activities that bring enjoyment. Unfortunately most of us never uncover our meaningful passions. They stay hidden.

Passions are more difficult to discover than gifts because they have to do with emotions and intuitive motives, but reflective response to the following questions can help:

- What do you enjoy talking about?
- If you knew you could not fail, what would you attempt?
- If resources were not a concern, what goals would you set?
- What do you daydream about doing?
- What would you like people to say at your funeral or to write on your gravestone?

Perhaps we don't know our passions, we are afraid of revealing them, or we don't know what to do with them. It may do us good to study more about discovering our destiny. Richard Nelson Bolles, who writes the annual edition of *What Color Is Your Parachute?* on job finding, wrote a gem of a small book called *How to Find Your Mission in Life.* This book really is the essence behind the more popular one but has been overlooked because mission and passion are sometimes not directly related to money-making and paying the bills. Mission relates to why you are here, what God has created you to do. Once you discover your mission in life, you must make it part of your life. If you cannot find a way to make a living by pursuing your mission, then you need to pursue your mission on the side. Pursue it as a hobby, something that occupies your energy before the family gets up in the morning, on your lunch break, after work, or late at night when everyone is in bed. Some people get started on their mission and then do what it takes to transform it into a career. Pastors commonly talk about their calling, referring to what they believe God has ordained them to do. Nonpastors, referring to the same thing, may talk about their vocation, which is a Latin word referring to voice (vocal), the voice of God in your life.

Prepare for Your Dreams

Pursuing inner callings requires some sort of preparation, whether it is physical, mental, spiritual, relational, or all of these. Too many people only dabble in what should be their most important life pursuits, their dreams. Do what it takes to immerse yourself in the area that interests you. Become an expert or learned student. Learn the needed skills. Develop your natural aptitudes.

Just now I talked to Jeff Fassero in a coffee shop where I write. Jeff attends our church and plays Major League baseball, formerly with the Mariners and Red Sox, now with the Cubs. Soon he is going to his former junior college in Springfield, Illinois, where they are retiring his number. Jeff has worked hard at pursuing his dream and does not let up just because he's made it. Between the busy seasons of over 160 games, he does not take it easy, watch TV, and eat candy bars. He's active working out and staying in shape. Jeff's natural ability to play baseball would not have amounted to much if he had not developed it over the years. And being unsatisfied with where he is, he continues to hone his skills. Discovered yet undeveloped talent rarely produces much.

Launch Boldly and Persevere

Quitting your day job may be foolish if you have to pay the rent, but take your calling—your dreams—seriously.

Few great accomplishments take place without sacrifice and perseverance. This may mean cutting back in areas that steal time and energy from the pursuit of your dream. You may need to reduce your social life, negotiate childcare, cancel your cable subscription, or get less sleep. Life has a way of expanding according to the time we make available. If you hope to put something else in your schedule, you'll need to take some things out and/or condense what's there. Quickly jump into your dream pursuits during this open time, before something else occupies the vacancy. Few vacuums exist in life. Stand strong. Lack of early rewards, negative support from friends, discouraging words from naysayers, and the common pull of procrastination will tempt you into relinquishing your dreams. Just assume that you'll be pretty much alone in your efforts early on. Like a rocket taking off, gravitational forces seek to hold the payload to the ground. The energy needed for orbiting is far less than that needed for launching.

Cheerlead

People who use their talents tend to appreciate seeing others utilizing theirs. When you notice that a person is good at something, encourage him or her to continue doing it. The more you can reinforce the mind-set in yourself and others that talents need to be used, not placed in a display case over the mantel, the more fulfilled you will feel. One of the teachings of the parable of the talents is to applaud others. If you are realizing your dream, the masses look on with jealous eyes as you sing the music written in your heart. They long for the faith in themselves and courage you express. Water the dreams of others. Fertilize the design of destiny. Little phrases such as, "You can do it," "Follow your dreams," "Don't let anyone deter you," and "I believe God has designed you for greatness," are all samples of how dream chasers can inspire others to do what they know they need to do in their hearts. The most unselfish thing you can do with your dreams is to let them inspire others to discover and follow their calling.

SELF-SABOTAGE ASSESSMENT

Place a value of 1 to 5 in the box beside each statement: 1 = no/rarely 2 = infrequently 3 = sometimes 4 = usually 5 = yes/always

- [ ] 1. I am confident that I've discovered my primary mission in life.
- [ ] 2. I am pleased with what I've accomplished thus far in life.
- [ ] 3. I know how I'm leaving my mark in the world.
- [ ] 4. I truly enjoy what I'm doing.
- [ ] 5. If I could live my life over, I'd want to do it the same.

Add the numbers and divide by 5. If your score is 1–2.5, you are probably being an enemy to yourself in this area. If your score is 2.6–3.75, you may want to consider this area more to see what is fuzzy or what you could do to improve it. If your score is over 3.75, you are either strong in this area or partially blind, which may require a perspective of someone who knows you well.

Self-sabotage assessment: _____

Another person's assessment of me: _____

UNPACKING PROCEDURES

1. What is one dream that you have pursued and accomplished?
2. What is one dream you've yet to pursue that others may or may not know about?
3. Can you think of someone who has buried his or her inner treasures and suffered as a result?
4. What is keeping you from pursuing your dream(s)?
5. If you could focus on two to seven life accomplishments, regardless of risk, pay, or peer pressure, what would you like to achieve or feel destined to pursue?
6. If I knew I could not fail, I'd attempt
   _____.

Fourteen

LOOKING BACK

I should never have moved out here. Things weren't so bad where I used to live. The job wasn't that great, but now we're all alone. I remember being able to eat dinner with the family, watch TV, or just go for a walk. Now, I'm so busy. Seems like we're never a family anymore. Back where we used to live, the kids had friends, parks to play in, and a great neighborhood. My folks drove me nuts at times, but at least we had somewhere to take the kids when we needed help. When we moved, we left our friends and our church. Things are so new and different here. What were we thinking? I guess the grass seemed greener. So we picked up and moved. Ugh, moving was a nightmare. I have no desire to do it again, but we did have it better than I thought. The pace of life now is ridiculous. There is so much going on all the time. With sports, homework, and the long commute, we never get to just hang out together. Well, if things don't work out here, I guess we can always go back.

Description and Dangers

The inability or unwillingness to move on is an attitude that cripples many people. Dwelling on the past can be either a fixation on a past hurt or failure or a fond memory of a wonderful experience that consumes our attention and grows even better over time. While today's culture can benefit from learning the importance of our heritage, savoring the past, and appreciating history, an inordinate amount of energy spent on the past is detrimental and self-sabotaging.

Do you have the following symptoms of focusing on the past?

1. You frequently refer to past friends and events.
2. You commonly wish you could go back to previous times.
3. You regret something you've done that prevents you from focusing on the future.

The Danger of Distorted Perceptions

Reading yesterday's newspaper does not keep today's problems from happening. While the mental VCR/DVD players can replay past experiences endlessly, our memories are not reality. They are perceived reality. We have not found any technology that allows for time travel, backward or forward. While memories can be wonderful, too much focus on them tends to distort our perceptions of our present and future life. When we respond to these distorted perceptions, we miss the mark, which in turn frustrates us. It is like looking at something underwater and reaching to grasp it. The water blurs our vision so that we do not see clearly.

We have all met people whose response to life was conditioned by a perspective that had been distorted by some past experience. Others, with sheltered past experiences, are unable to muster the energy to cope with present difficulties. Those with harsh pasts are often pessimistic, defensive, or fearful of present opportunities. Living in the past plays with our emotions and does not equip us for current realities.

The Danger of Looking Behind Us

Fixed to the windshields of cars are small rearview mirrors. We use these to see if anything is coming up behind us, to be sure that all is clear before backing up, or to check on the kids in the backseat. But notice how small the rearview mirror is compared to the windshield. It's tiny in comparison. The reason for this is that cars are designed primarily to go forward, not backward. When we try to drive our lives forward by looking in the rearview mirror, we're going to run into things. We will crash into bills, work, relationships, and potential opportunities, because we're not watching for them. Our attention is on the past.

Several years ago, a young woman I know was killed by a reckless driver. At first, her parents were very forgiving and amazingly gracious toward the irresponsible man. But a few months later, the father and mother began to become angry and vindictive. They mourned the loss of their daughter. A few years later, I learned that this couple had all but given up on God and life itself. They could not get over the loss of their child and the bitterness they felt toward the driver. Their marriage was strained and they had become very unhappy people.

When pain comes our way, we embrace it, but then we must let it go. When we do not, we make the loss much bigger than it really is, and we give up what we could have gained by trusting God to take us through our suffering.

The Danger of Being Left Behind

When we focus on past events, good or bad, we tend to be left behind by the rest of the world, which is going forward. Life has a way of moving us, from house to house, job to job, and even friend to friend. If we cling to yesterday, those who keep the pace with today move away from us. People who are future oriented will be even farther ahead of us. We don't have to go anywhere to alienate ourselves. By staying right where we're at, the rest of the world will move on without us.

This behavitude initially sounds like a contradiction to the "Have Bags, Will Travel" behavitude in chapter 9. Actually, it is the bipolar opposite. The person who cannot stay in one place or relationship for long has an inner problem of restlessness and an insatiable appetite for greener grass. Unable to find inner contentment, the person seeks external improvements. Conversely, the "Looking Back" behavitude reflects a person who suffers from root rot, fearful of the new and unknown and therefore clinging to what is familiar, comfortable, and predictable. Both behavitudes are unhealthy and self-sabotaging.

Living in the past works against our emotional, intellectual, and spiritual growth. And it makes it difficult for those who are moving forward to relate to us. People who are into self-improvement and personal growth cannot afford to stay where they are. While they may still love those of us who stay behind, they will be in a different point in life and will find it increasingly difficult to relate to and enjoy us. That is why family and school reunions are so often strained—some people are moving into the future while others are locked into a time warp.

The Danger of Overestimating the Benefits of the Past

"When I was a kid, we walked barefoot in the snow, to and from school, three miles, uphill both ways." It's quite interesting how our minds have a way of playing tricks on us. "The good ol' days" to my grandparents were the Depression years and World War II. My parents had nothing close to the creature comforts and benefits that my family experiences, but they sometimes refer to the past as "the good ol' days."

Funny how years have a way of distorting our perspectives in a negative as well as a positive direction. We remember how difficult life was growing up, but we forget the good times we had. I can tell you many stories about farm life in the Midwest as an only child, working long hours in the freezing dead of winter. We had to feed the cows in the middle of ice storms and blizzards, warming our hands on the exhaust manifold of the tractor. Those difficult times make their way into my speeches and fatherly lectures more often than tales of fishing, horseback riding, and playing in the haystack. To most of us, the past is convenient fodder for supporting all kinds of justifications for our feelings and behavior.

Because of our mind's ability to filter out most hurts, however, the tendency is for us to overemphasize the benefits of the past, while overestimating the challenges of the present. There is no pain like present pain. Most pain has a short life and diminishes over time, at least in intensity. By focusing on our perceptions of the past, we build up excuses for not facing our current challenges. Telling ourselves that the past was so much better diminishes our motivation to tackle the problems of the present. We get discouraged and may remain stuck where we are because we can't go back but we are unwilling to move forward.

The Lure of the Past

Why do we focus on the past when to do so is self-defeating? Here are four reasons:

1. *The past is familiar and thus causes less stress.* New and unfamiliar situations create stress. The familiar means we don't have to change; we can predict what will happen, good or bad. When we are stressed in other parts of our lives, we are tempted to spend an

unhealthy amount of time fantasizing about the past, whether it is about previous jobs, friends, lovers, homes, or settings. Thus, by dwelling in the past, we seemingly maintain the peace of mind that we desire.

Pursuing peace and avoiding stress are not necessarily the same process. We do not gain tranquillity by sticking our head in the sand. Trying to ignore what's going on around us can be as stressful as facing it. Pain management is the name of the game, and we try to do it primarily via avoidance. For the most part, short-term fantasies are not bad, but when they keep us from dealing with present responsibilities, they can be detrimental.

When we follow a well-worn route, we avoid the hassles of blazing a new trail. We like the familiar. We've been this way before. Even if it is out of the way and longer, we repeat it. Even if it caused us problems in the past, still it's something we know. This is one reason why people repeat the same mistakes, remarry similar spouses, and do not seem to break out of self-destructive decisions. The things of the past are familiar and seem less threatening than the untried and unfamiliar.

2. *We are controlled by our guilt and remorse.* We think by clinging to the past we can somehow go back and change things. All of us have unfinished business from the past. We've made mistakes; we've said and done things we regret. Perhaps we were too hard on a child or we kick ourselves for not accepting a job offer or we passed up on the perfect house. Second-guessing is tough on us. Hindsight has a way of beating us up. By pondering the past, we somehow believe that we can relive it and thus undo the misdeed or correct the bad decision. Obviously we realize this is impossible when we're in our right mind, but reminiscing feeds our hope.

We may be realistic about the impossibility of reliving the past, but we may still be trapped in the desire for a second chance. But even second chances are not repeat first chances. The river we step into tomorrow is different from the one we messed up in today. Circumstances change. People are not the same. We can learn from the past and make better decisions tomorrow because of it, but we cannot undo what has been done and we cannot go back. Though we replay yesterday's game film over and over, we cannot change the score. Instead, we can grow from the past and learn from it, but we can't expect to change it.

3. *We convince ourselves that we can avoid future shock by hanging on to yesterday.* The future can be a very scary place. While opportunities provide incredible potential, the possibility for failure is big as well. So much is happening so fast. We can feel what Alvin Toffler described in his book *Future Shock.* Feeling caught in the crosshairs of reality and should-be is nerve-racking. What does the future hold as information doubles every few months? When will I be rendered obsolete? What if the Internet crashes or the economy implodes? What will I be doing in the next twenty years and will I have the skill or brainpower to be marketable? With every new opportunity comes a new set of concerns, requirements, and possibilities for success as well as failure. We're beyond the optimistic/pessimistic question, Is the glass half full or half empty? It is both full and empty and we have to deal with these conflicting realities at the same time. So we find that there is one way to deal with the threat of future shock and that is to relive the past. Granted, it does not solve anything, but it provides a temporary shelter from the onslaught of technology and uncertainty. Sometimes we just get tired

of dealing with today. Sometimes we just want to curl up and suck on yesterday's thumb. While most of us realize this is no cure for our present anxiety, it's comforting when we can retreat to what's familiar.

4. *We haven't accomplished anything recently so we try to rest on past laurels.* Scottsdale has a number of retired sports professionals. These people are not decrepit, just too old for pro sports. One NBA acquaintance has the license plate HAS BEEN on his vehicle. Some of the lesser-known athletes meld into the community like any other citizen. The celebrity types still get recognized, but not like before. Few fans ask about recent ventures, focusing instead on past glory.

This may be true of most of us—our past was more glorious than is our present. Whether it was youthful sports accomplishments, being prom queen, valedictorian, or various work or volunteer awards, we're tempted to focus on those times. There is nothing like hearing the applause, being blinded by the limelight, and feeling the warmth of affirmation.

If our self-image has been inordinately constructed around past highlights, we're tempted to revisit them and find in them our identity. When who we are is based on who we were, we run the risk of avoiding the future by living in the past. Someone said success is like a sword. You can do a lot of things with it except sit on it.

Becoming Your Own Best Ally

Anticipate the Future

People are hope-seekers. They will look for hope wherever they can find it. That is why people get fooled by scams, con artists, and dysfunctional relationships. When we lack hope in our lives, we're tempted to focus on past hope because past hope is better than no hope at all. Past hope is really an oxymoron, because the orientation of hope is future. When we accomplish something we hope for, there is no longer a need for hope. Past hope that is realized is hope's fulfillment. "But hope that is seen is no hope at all. Who hopes for what he already has? But if we hope for what we do not yet have, we wait for it patiently" (Rom. 8:24–25). What is something new you anticipate? What is a dream you have? What can you do today to work toward this dream? Imagine the excitement of realizing your dream and accomplishing a goal. Anticipate something good in the future.

Seek Professional Counsel

If you have experienced a trauma in your past, you may need professional help to let it go. Significant past experiences are sometimes sticky, adhering to our emotions and memories. Like lint and static cling during a Midwest winter, they attach themselves to our thoughts again, even though we try to push the memories away. If you have never sought professional help because of the stigma of talking to a "shrink," think of the counselor as an attitude consultant, a relationship coach, or a mind expert. We're more and more familiar with these terms and pretty much, that's what the good ones are. There are no magic wands or pixie dust available. You must be the hero if you are to get better. We all need a little help to make it through life. When past events loom large in our memories, we need some emotional Preparation H to shrink the swelling. This remedy is far better than drugs, serial affairs, alcohol, or other self-destructive behaviors.

Remember to Forget

Forgetting in life is not always automatic. Sometimes it has to be intentional. You may find it helpful to create a ritual to formally bury the past, good or bad. As a pastor, I have the opportunity to participate in, as well as to officiate at, a number of life milestones. Weddings, baby dedications, baptisms, commencement services, and funerals are the most common. Sometimes I'm amazed by the amounts of time, money, and energy that go into these ceremonies. People take them very seriously. Why is this? One reason people invest energy in big events like marriages, births, and deaths is to make the occasion memorable.

You can make a special occasion out of the choice to put the past behind you. By creating your own ceremony, you make it a point in time, which will have an enduring effect, even though the event itself is brief. By creating your own memorial, you are marking the past, allowing you to progress. Whether it's to commemorate the ending of a marriage or business, to plant a tree or raise a flag in memory of a loved one, or just throw a party for a grand accomplishment and display the memorabilia, make it a memorable time. Invite friends over; have a plaque made; take pictures.

If someone has offended you, write a note to forgive or tell off the person and then burn it in the fireplace. Symbolically remove the item from your "to do" list. There are many ways we can intentionally honor and revere what has happened, good or bad, as well as mark its passing. Assume you're going to have to let the past go again and again.

Establish Boundaries

Just because your focus needs to be forward, you don't have to totally forget the past. If it's all or nothing, you may not wish to leave the past. For example, if your focus on the past is a lost loved one, you may feel that you are dishonoring him or her by moving ahead. You feel like a traitor to the memory of your loved one who died. But letting go does not mean forgetting. You can take flowers to the grave periodically, talk about the person in conversations, and pay respect without becoming fixated. The difference between honoring the past and living there is that when you simply honor it, your primary focus is on the present and the future.

You cannot change the past, but you can learn from it and appreciate it. Reality in this world means you cannot go back and relive yesterday. Trying to do it in your mind is virtual reality, far from the truth. Plan what seems to be an honorable balance and then stick to it. Fight the urge to linger longer in memories. For example, if you want to place flowers by a grave, do it the first Saturday of every month and no more. By planning how you will honor the past, you will be better able to keep it from spilling out inordinately into your present. Then you are free from the guilt of not remembering and still at liberty to deal with today. Welcoming the future involves saying good-bye to yesterday.

SELF-SABOTAGE ASSESSMENT

Place a value of 1 to 5 in the box beside each statement: 1 = no/rarely 2 = infrequently 3 = sometimes 4 = usually 5 = yes/always

☐ 1. I spend most of my time dealing with the present and future.

☐ 2. I consider the things that happened in my past
over.

☐ 3. I am excited about what lies ahead in my life.

☐ 4. I think only occasionally of past victories.

☐ 5. I avoid pondering regrets I have about the past.

Add the numbers and divide by 5. If your score is
1–2.5, you are probably being an enemy to yourself
in this area. If your score is 2.6–3.75, you may want
to consider this area more to see what is fuzzy or what
you could do to improve it. If your score is over 3.75,
you are either strong in this area or partially blind,
which may require a perspective of someone who
knows you well.

Self-sabotage assessment: _____

Another person's assessment of me: _____

UNPACKING PROCEDURES

1. What are two or three high points in your past?
Why were these memorable events?

2. What are two or three low points in your past?
Why were these memorable events?

3. Have any of the events from questions one and
two seemed to become focal points that consume
a lot of your present energy?

4. Do you know someone who has had a difficult or
wonderful past, who seems to do a good job living in the present and future?

5. Do you know someone who suffers from looking
back? Why do you think he or she is fixated on

the past? What do you think he or she is missing out on because of this behavitude?

6. What, if anything, seems to be keeping you from enjoying today?

7. What, if anything, seems to be holding you back from a hopeful future?

Fifteen

QUICK AND EASY

So I tell the salesman, "This is too much money. There is no way we can afford this car right now. I work on commission and sales have been slow lately. My wife is wanting to quit her job so she can stay home and raise our children."

So we go through the normal haggling and he comes back with this incredibly low monthly lease payment. "How does this sound?" he asks. Now all the while, I know what he's doing. I'm in sales. But I look at my old car, and then the new one, and I think to myself, *I can do this. We can handle it. We'll eat out a few times less and I'll work harder at selling.*

So, we drive off the lot in our brand-new car. I'll tell you, the first few months were wonderful. We showed it off to our friends, who loved it. The neighbors came over and drooled on it. But then, my selling didn't pick up like I'd hoped. Now, three years later, the car is having a few problems. My wife has not been able to quit work because of our other bills. We argue about the silliest things, but I think it's stress-related because of our tight finances. The car doesn't seem nearly as special as it used to, just another purchase.

Description and Dangers

We live in a fast-paced world. One of my favorite magazines is *Fast Company*. But every time I finish reading it, I initially feel a bit depressed. I get the sense that I'm not keeping up, that I'm falling behind because I'm not going faster and faster. We don't have time to read the fine print, cover all the bases, or wait for our savings to accrue. So we make hasty decisions, base purchases on monthly affordability, and sign off our souls to the gods of easy payments. While "quick and easy" things are tempting, the cumulative effect of indulging in them is frightening.

Do you have the following symptoms of going for what is quick and easy?

1. You have made a series of sudden but significant decisions that have not panned out as you thought they would, creating stress in your life.
2. You have increasing debt because of purchases you have made on the spur of the moment.
3. You have a few big regrets because you acted against your gut and/or others' recommendations.

The Danger of Short-Term Joy

Buyer's remorse refers to what we feel when we fail to do our homework before making a purchase and wind up with a lemon or a less than satisfactory commitment. While in graduate school, we saw an ad for a used Mazda RX-7 sports car. The price seemed too good to be true. We called the phone number of a man who ran a small used-car lot and an auto body shop.

Like most graduate students, we were barely surviving financially, but our lack of overhead made living on the edge enticing. We shelled out the money and were the proud owners of a cool, little sports car. But within a few days, we noticed that the steering wheel was very stiff. Whenever we ran the car at highway speeds, it would vibrate. We called up the dealer and asked him if this was normal with this kind of car. He said that all sports cars are a little bumpy on the road. After a few more weeks, we knew something was wrong. We took the car to a different mechanic and he told us it had obviously been in a wreck and had some permanent damage. When we called up the dealer, he denied fooling us but pointed out the "as is" clause in the sales agreement. We were stuck.

Most of us can think of similar early learning-curve illustrations. Buyer beware. But when we fail to be diligent, we'll often suffer the consequences.

The Danger of Debt Strangulation

The recent Sears ad in my mail showed gleaming new appliances. In bold print were the monthly payments. Who couldn't afford twenty-nine dollars a month for a top-of-the-line washer? In small print was the total price, cash outright, without tax or credit card interest rates. QVC shopping channel shows off its current offering, asking three payments of only thirty-nine dollars each, operators standing by. The car dealer's question is, "How much do you want to spend a month?" With credit card solicitors, convenient, seemingly miniscule payments, and an endless stream of goods and services dangled in front of our eyes, getting into debt has never been easier. Most of us in our thirties are in our acquisition stage, having a family, purchasing a house, decorating it, and trying to establish our household. Knowing when, where, and how to stop buying is very difficult. "Just one more" becomes our motto as we seek to make it happen. For a while, the wind blowing through our hair is fun. The hope, hunt, and have trilogy is exhilarating. No one can deny it. But after the sheen wears off, the bills continue. Money is the number one reason behind marital fights. Debts are the cause of many divorces, bankruptcies, and long-term enslavement to creditors. Yet salesmen do not put guns to our heads, forcing us into deals we were unwilling to close.

The Danger of Missing Out on Better Deals

When we are overly committed, we automatically preclude better options down the road. Like the popular song laments, "I married and then the right one came along." When today we use up our present and future resources, we are not able to take advantage of good deals tomorrow. Obviously, if you never commit, you'll never have. But a rush to have too soon leads to incredible remorse when you have to pass up on a sale, an important relationship, or a better home. During these times of regret, you may be tempted to pass the buck, take your disappointment out on those around you, and even curse God. But behind all the smoke and mirrors is usually one person who is most to blame for this dilemma—you.

When I was a senior in college, I was engaged to a cute, nice woman. Even though I loved her, I never felt total peace about our relationship. I thought there might be someone else who better fit the image of the person I'd marry. But no one else came along; friends and family provided encouragement, so I assumed she was the right one. To make a long story short, we postponed the wedding because I was accepted to spend the summer in the Caribbean for a mission trip. On that ministry team was the girl I'd always imagined marrying. Needless to say, I painfully ended the engagement and married my dream girl teammate a year later. I've met many people who identify with my story. Often, though, the outcome for them was not as happy because they denied their gut reactions.

The Danger of Causing Stress for Others

One of the problems of mismanaging our resources is that the effects often create secondary stress. When we pack more baggage than we can carry, other people usually end up picking up the slack. Children from previous bad marriages, lingering effects of bankruptcy, and emotional scars become the problems of those we associate with down the road. The stress of this baggage often becomes burdensome and strains healthy relationships. This in turn depletes our joy. Thus we end up bearing first and subsequent effects of our bad choices. Just a few years of counseling others would give you a pretty good perspective of the many lives that have compounded stress because of a series of poor choices. Each new negative outcome tends to increase the burden.

Living on the Edge

Why do we make quick and easy decisions when it's self-defeating? Here are four reasons:

1. *We get caught in the sucker syndrome.* Circus marketer P. T. Barnum said, "A sucker is born every day." Let's be very honest as well as nonjudgmental when we say, some people just have more street smarts than others. If you've not been blessed with an ability either to know intuitively or to learn quickly that everything that glitters is not gold, you're going to become one of Barnum's suckers. If you're not blessed with this ability, there will be people who will take advantage of you. Perhaps the best resolution to this problem is simply to know your limitations. Setting up preestablished parameters allows you to rest on your standards, not your feelings.

   If you're a feeling-oriented person, chances are good that you have unique gifts that others do not. You may be very trusting of people, loving, affirming, and selfless. But when it comes to developing relationships or making important purchases, you're going to be handicapped. Just as physically and mentally challenged people have barriers they have to overcome, you have your own. Naïveté and gullibility are hindrances when it comes to making fast decisions on deals that seem too good to be true. Other people who are prone to the sucker syndrome are the lazy or overly busy. When you don't want to put in the effort to do background checks and read *Consumer Reports* or the fine print, you're opening yourself up to problems. Smart, otherwise shrewd people can become suckers when they make decisions on the run. When life is a blur, we can't discern what is and is not a good deal. The ability to slow down and ponder the pros and cons is vital to making good choices. "I didn't bother to . . ." is a common lament among those who shoot themselves in the foot.

2. *We suffer from insecurity.* When we need the affection of other people, we are apt to do whatever it takes to get that attention. How many women have gone to bed with men other than their husbands, because they wanted to be loved? We men can be horribly shallow, flying by the fly of our pants, in many cases. Some of us are apt to tell women whatever they want to hear, so that we can get whatever we want from them. While this sounds hugely sexist, it is reality and the cause behind a lot of the pain I see in people.

When a person gets dumped, cheated on, or divorced, there is a strong temptation to jump immediately into another relationship. The rebound effect is very real. Rarely does this relationship, or any within the first year, turn out to be healthy and lasting. When we hurry into commitments that we'll soon regret, we're being driven by our sense of insecurity. Before long the person who rushes into a relationship discovers that being single and unhappy for years is better than being unhappy with another person for a few weeks.

No one makes us enter these less than optimum relationships. No man forces a woman to go to bed with him (outside of rape).

I usually begin my premarital counseling by saying, "You can tell a young man in love, but you can't tell him much." Most people are not very objective when it comes to love, and yet choosing a mate is the most important life decision we will make. When we feel insecure alone, we're prone to jumping into relationships faster and deeper than we ought, thus setting ourselves up for pain.

3. *We have bad brakes.* Instant gratification is our enemy, not our friend. The inability to put our hormones, wants, or needs on hold creates big problems. That's a tough thing to do. Even the proverb admits that "hope deferred makes the heart sick" (Prov. 13:12). We gratify to feel good for the moment but buy big regrets as a result.

When the brakes on your car are bad, you'd better not tailgate or drive too fast in bad conditions, because you'll have an accident. When our self-discipline is not what it should be, that's the equivalent of bad brakes. We'll run into bad purchases, relationships, and time commitments, and we'll have the bumps and bruises to show for them.

Self-denial is not a popular concept among marketers because they know that if people have to sleep on a sale before making a decision, they are more apt to say no. If you ever read "today only" in the verbiage, it's a sign that you're about to become a sucker. If the deal is so good, it should be there tomorrow. Impulse buying is the root of most buyers' remorse. If you know you're prone to want it now, take a friend or family member who is more disciplined, who can help you apply the brakes. Make a family deal that purchases over a certain amount require both you and your spouse to agree, or that you'll always sleep on deals over five hundred dollars or so.

None of us has perfect brakes. We may have grown up with parents who had their emergency brakes on all the time, so now that we are adults, we overdo our freedom of choice. Overdone freedom becomes a self-induced prison. Get your brakes fixed.

4. *We want to keep up with the Joneses and we settle for near-sighted living.* Nearsighted people have a hard time seeing things in the distance. But the far-off represents our future, where we're going to be down the road. Because we are social beings and influenced both good and bad by other people, we seldom make choices in a vacuum. What people wear, where they eat, what they drive, where they live, all become cues that influence us. When we identify with a certain group of people, we strive to emulate them all the more.

The irony is that groups such as youth or gangs strive to rebel against society, but they create even more restrictive conformity within their group. Members have far stricter standards than those outside the groups.

Regardless, none of us is as independent as we think, and while we're not independent of influence, we're still responsible for our decisions. Thus, when we decide to do what others are doing, we can sabotage ourselves. Driving a status car, wearing a designer label, buying a certain home, and joining a popular fitness club can stretch us beyond our limits.

Ironically we live our lives to impress people we often don't like or even know. Who are these Joneses who so dramatically influence us? They are neighbors, work associates, and relatives. We want to prove to our father-in-law that we are not the failure he thought when we married his daughter. We want to prove to our demanding parent that we did amount to something after all. We try to impress our associates with how well we're doing, all the while digging ourselves deeper into debt and stress. When people say, "I'm my own person," it means they're either a sociopath or a liar. None of us is fully our own person if we live within the normal ranks of society. But when an inordinate amount of our self-image and sense of worth is based on external comparisons, we're governed by what others do and feel we must acquire things as fast as we are able. Deferred gratification creates huge internal conflict when our self-esteem is externally oriented.

Becoming Your Own Best Ally

No Free Lunches

How many times do you have to hear the cliché "There are no free lunches"? But the idea of a free lunch, no strings attached, tempts each new generation.

> Go to the ant, you sluggard; consider its ways and be wise! It has no commander, no overseer or ruler, yet it stores its provisions in summer and gathers its food at harvest. How long will you lie there, you sluggard? When will you get up from your sleep? A little sleep, a little slumber, a little folding of the hands to rest—and poverty will come on you like a bandit and scarcity like an armed man.
>
> Proverbs 6:6–11

Albert Einstein said that the most intriguing mystery of the world is "compounding interest." If you were to double a dollar every year, it takes only twenty years to turn a dollar into over a million. But after ten years, you have only a little over a thousand. It's so tempting at that point to look at the account and empty it for the next appliance, car down payment, or vacation. When you do this, you have to start all over toward your goal of a million. When you empty that account, it's going to cost you.

While the things that mean most in life cannot be bought with money, everything, purchased or otherwise, will cost you something. Nothing worthwhile is free or easy. Some might say, "That's an interesting thing for a pastor to say. Don't you believe in grace, unmerited favor? Certainly that's free." Yes, but free does not mean cheap or necessarily easy. Someone had to pay the price. According to the Bible, that was God, giving us the life of his Son.

Too Good to Be True

"If it's too good to be true, it probably is." The Post Office poster sums it up well. Mail fraud, incredible deals, not wanting to miss out on a steal, and the urge to look better than we really are create opportunities for us to fritter away our resources. After so much frittering, we are left with disappointment, a handful of invoices, and diminished esteem because of our bad judgment.

We take a job because it seems so wonderful, but when we get there, we realize it's been billed as far better than it is, so we quit and look for something else. After so many moves and embarrassing explanations, we assume that it would be better to start over in some other place. Part of the high mobility within our society is due to the desire for fresh starts after many poor decisions. Instead of learning how to avoid these pitfalls, we hope a new environment will help us start over.

Don't become a cynic, but if too many things seem too good to be true, then you probably need to stop and do some further research. As a newlywed, I remember purchasing a set of nonstick pans advertised on television. The price fit our budget. When we got them, they appeared to be Teflon-coated tin foil. What a joke! Salesmen and marketers specialize in making their wares seem perfect. When they accomplish this, chances are there will be a flood of buyer's remorse.

Consider the Long View

Healthy eyesight gives us good perspectives, within reason, from both close and far range. As a midlifer, it's kind of funny to see peers holding their reading materials at full arm's length and finally giving up and donning their reading glasses. I suppose it's humorous because I've not yet had to do it. When we realize our eyesight is less than 20/20, we compensate by how we hold our reading materials or we buy contacts or glasses.

If you discover that you are inherently nearsighted in your decision-making, then consciously considering the long view is essential to avoiding quick and easy choices you'll regret. What will be the total cost, interest included, after the loan is paid off? What will you have to give up down the road if you acquire this now? What if the commission check does not come through? Most of us know at least one person who is so incredibly long viewed that he or she is no fun. But most of us need not fear this state. Risks are a part of life, but risky ventures can ruin marriages and friendships and can unnecessarily stress life in general. When you do not consider the long view, you become your own worst enemy.

Seek Counsel

When I go to dinner with one of my reading-glasses-dependent friends, he may ask, "What does this say? I left my reading glasses at home." Because he trusts me, I can tell him what the menu says. If you have a difficult time with the long view, consider the views of others, especially those you trust. Were they happy with a similar purchase? What would a money manager advise? What do the experts say? Obviously, whom you trust is key. Avoid relying on someone who is trying to sell you something. Regardless of his or her motives, when a person is making a bonus or commission on your purchase, it will bias his or her advice.

Most of us have never been taught to budget, invest, or make responsible fiscal decisions. One of the best things parents can do for their children is to prepare them in this area. Because this rarely happens, most of us begin with a liability. We're vulnerable to the advertising schemes so prevalent in our capitalistic culture. So do your homework and seek the counsel of discerning friends, not just any friends.

SELF-SABOTAGE ASSESSMENT

Place a value of 1 to 5 in the box beside each statement: 1 = no/rarely 2 = infrequently 3 = sometimes 4 = usually 5 = yes/always

☐ 1. I research a subject (brand/model/financing) before a major purchase.

☐ 2. I have a rule that I will sleep on a decision to purchase an item over five hundred dollars (or some other set amount).

☐ 3. I tend to look at the long-term effects of a decision before making it.

☐ 4. I seek professional and/or spiritual counsel before making a big decision.

☐   5. I can think of several times when I said no to purchases or relationships because I did not feel good about them.

Add the numbers and divide by 5. If your score is 1–2.5, you are probably being an enemy to yourself in this area. If your score is 2.6–3.75, you may want to consider this area more to see what is fuzzy or what you could do to improve it. If your score is over 3.75, you are either strong in this area or partially blind, which may require a perspective of someone who knows you well.

Self-sabotage assessment: _____

Another person's assessment of me: _____

UNPACKING PROCEDURES

1. What is an example of a decision you regret because it was quick and/or easy? What did you learn from this?
2. How do you think peers and associates influence your purchases? (If you say not at all, that's apt to be a blind spot.)
3. Can you think of anyone who has made a huge mistake in a purchase or relationship because he or she did not do the needed homework? What would be your advice to this person for the next time?
4. When are you most vulnerable to making a bad decision? Where are your weaknesses (e.g., cars,

clothes, bargains, Internet shopping, shopping channel, charging)?

5. What part of your fiscal education needs to be expanded? What can you do to augment this?

6. What kind of spiritual wisdom do you seek on a consistent basis? How do you know it is reliable?

7. What have you learned about reading people who want to sell you something or themselves? How could you get help in learning how to be more discerning?

Sixteen

BUMP SIGNS

You know, I have half a mind to smack him up side the head. Sometimes he makes me so mad. But then, I've always had a temper, you know. Think about it. I was born with red hair, am part Irish, and was a middle child to boot. My dad left the family when I was twelve and my mom had to work two jobs just to keep food on the table. It's no wonder I am the way I am. I can't help myself. I've learned that if you want to survive, you have to be tough. You can't take guff off of anyone. When you add to that my personality temperament, you're dealing with nitroglycerin. I know I may be a little rough around the edges, but given my circumstances, it's a good thing for other people that I'm not worse.

Description and Dangers

Growing up on a farm meant I commuted to school, long before I ever heard the word *commuter*. The ride was forty-five minutes each way. In the Midwest, spring brings potholes, created by water that seeps under the road, soil that sinks, and ice that creates cracks in the pavement. I remember one stretch of road on the way to Macksburg Elementary that was especially rough. The road crew put up a sign that read "Bump" before one big pothole, to warn drivers of the potential danger. The bump was a doosie, and after a few weeks, it was still there—along with the sign. Over a year later, the road had still not been fixed. It was as if putting up the sign fulfilled the repairmen's responsibility. They didn't need to fix it; just read the sign, drivers.

This describes a self-defeating behavitude, which is quite popular. Instead of fixing a problem, we merely label it, recognize it for what it is, and even make a public announcement about it. Perhaps the popularity of psychology has encouraged this behavior, for today we are more aware of our neuroses than ever. To some, having a therapist is akin to having a nice home and car. Never before have we been so able to understand our inner self. But for many people, merely identifying problems seems to be sufficient, giving them a license to behave irresponsibly.

Do you have the following symptoms of using labels to identify problems that you don't intend to do anything about?

1. You know all the psychological jargon and are good at diagnosing problems but you don't know how to fix them.
2. You label people and treat them according to stereotypes.
3. You talk about your ills, challenges, and goals, but you never do anything about them.

The Danger of False Assumptions

Many people are broadcasting ideas, but ideas and truth are two different things. When we fail to investigate, uncover the facts, and take the time to verify what is true, we run the risk of making false assumptions. One example is the ridiculous mottoes and one-liners that accompany propositions around election time. I am writing this section just before a major election. We are inundated with hundreds of messages that tell us what is best for us. Unless we take the time to read the fine print and ask educated insiders, we're apt to vote for the person with the nicest signs, the cutest motto, or the most recognized endorsements.

This weakness is behind the bump sign behavitude, when people merely label and describe without getting explanations or investigating more deeply. We make overarching assumptions to which we attach one-word descriptions. Usually, after giving a problem a name, we avoid the work of fixing it. We assume we understand the details because we have been able to label it. This can prove to be a foolish assumption.

The Danger of Confusing Circumstances with Causes

One thing that researchers teach us is that you cannot assume a causal relationship just because two things occur at the same time. For example, if a superstitious baseball player hits a home run and later discovers his underwear is inside-out, he'll begin to intentionally wear his boxers tag-side-out at every game. While this is not logical, he believes there may have been some causal relationship between his brilliant performance and the inside-out undies. In a similar fashion, we can say that we are second-born, choleric, born on the wrong side of the tracks or use any number of other descriptors and draw conclusions as to why we're hard to live with, a jerk, lazy, overweight, mean, or mediocre. "Because I'm this or that, don't expect me to . . ."

I wonder—is it the bump signs that make the bumps in the roads? Think about it! Whenever you see a sign, sure enough, there's a bump! Which comes first, the bump or the bump sign? We could ask the same question about our personality quirks. Are we hard to get along with because our parents fought all the time when we were growing up? Or are we using our dysfunctional family as an excuse for our poor behavior? While we cannot ignore childhood influences, temperament, and so on, it's far too easy to use our circumstances as reasons for why we can't do better. The danger in drawing these improper conclusions is that we set ourselves up for failure and cap the limit of our willpower.

The Danger of Labeling Ourselves

The problem with plentiful bump signs is that we can easily find a few that describe our weaknesses and then proceed to use them as a license for acting out our shortcomings instead of fixing them. By informing people that we're from a dysfunctional family, have red hair, are type A, a middle child, or any number of other labels, we feel free to be impatient, snide, and unloving.

Sometimes we engage the Pygmalion effect and become what others see us to be. When others see us in a negative light, we behave that way. Since taking the path of least resistance is always the easiest, we run the risk of living out of our weaknesses. When we behave unlovingly toward others, they become hurt and offended and end up pulling back from us. This in turn hurts us because we lose our friends, family, and work associates. By acting out our bump signs instead of fixing the problem, we perpetuate them. "That's just the way I am. Love me or leave me."

When we announce to others the way we are, we think it absolves us of the responsibility for how we treat others. Sometimes we assume that because others seem to accept our assessment of ourselves, we have the right to continue in our immaturity.

We may be a professional success but if we mistreat others and find excuses for it, we're immature. Stories abound of talented, powerful people who throw tantrums on the movie set or in the boardroom, ranting and raving like lunatics and abusing people all the while. These insecure despots can always find enough weak people to bully or needy people who hang around them because of what they can provide in terms of money, power, and position. So they never feel the need to grow up.

The Danger of Labeling Others

When you give people the once-over and label them along ethnic, gender, and personality stereotypes, you run the risk of grossly misunderstanding them and neglecting some potentially great friends and associates. First impressions are lasting ones, but they are not necessarily reliable.

Remember the Titans is a wonderful movie that illustrates the danger of prejudice and bias. When the football team was first integrated in the 1960s, the players brought many preconceived ideas about each other. If they hadn't learned to get rid of their racial prejudice, they would never have won the championship.

Ethnicity is but one of many label types that we pin on people, but these labels do little to help us understand them. In fact, the labels hinder our getting to know others because they act as walls that keep us separate. Labels may summarize education, nation or region of the country of origin, gender, temperament, wealth, neighborhood, organizational role, height, weight, attire, and beauty, but they never give us in-depth insight into who a person is. Labels are prejudgments, which is the meaning of prejudice. Prejudice is summing up a person on the basis of superficial factors, without getting to know him or her. When we do this, we fail to treat each individual as the unique person he or she is.

Using Labels

Why do we put up bump signs that work against us and hurt others? Here are four reasons:

1. *Pop psychology has taught us in part to become aware of our faults, often without showing us how to fix them.* Partial knowledge can be a detriment. The saying "I know enough to be dangerous" has a lot of truth to it. The plethora of books, talk shows, and magazine articles that help us understand the depths of the human psyche in seven easy steps are often very informative. But our knowledge of terms and concepts often outweighs our ability to implement the ideas. I see this constantly in church life, when people's knowledge about God far exceeds their experience of God and obedience to his ways.

   When I meet a high school or college sophomore, I have fun asking him if he knows the literal meaning of the word *sophomore*. It comes from two Greek words, *sophos,* which means wise and from which we get our word *sophisticated,* and *moros,* which is the root word of *moron.* Literally it means sophisticated moron. When you are a freshman, you know you're a moron and so do others. You're green, learning the ropes, a rookie—in school, work, and sports. But when you're a sophomore, you think you're experienced and competent and you flaunt it. Actually you're still a freshman—with one year of experience—so in essence you've become a sophisticated moron.

   When we understand a bit of psychology as well as our own strengths and weaknesses, we are often just a few steps ahead of where we were—a sophisticated moron—but we think we are enlightened, experienced, and wise.

2. *By acknowledging that our shortcomings exist, we appear to be well-informed, enlightened, and even self-actualized.*

As we've seen, one of the reasons behind this behavitude is ignorance of how to improve. Another has more to do with flaunting our weaknesses to appear cool. Getting to know yourself is an assumed requirement of modern living. You're not with it unless you have a grasp of your strengths and weaknesses. Although pride keeps some people from sharing their weaknesses, others seem almost to take pride in their shortcomings. Going to a psychologist for counseling used to be a hushed secret. Now you can hear people in coffee shops publicly announcing what their therapist told them. Accepting the need for good mental and behavioral coaching is a positive. But identifying and accepting problems are merely the first two steps, albeit vital ones, in accomplishing growth. I see an increasing number of people hiding behind these smoke screens.

3. *We fail to understand that confession carries with it the responsibility to make changes.* Reason one for this behavitude is that we lack knowledge of how to change. The second reason is that declaring our weaknesses seems the enlightened thing to do. A third reason is that we confuse confession with the complex process and hard work of correction.

My wife asks me if I know how to cook. I tell her that I used to cook some growing up, but I loathed the cleanup. Making a mess is much easier and even more fun than cleaning up the mess. Acknowledging things in our lives that need repair is far easier than fixing them. Personal growth is difficult work. Even the most dedicated person can grow weary at times of the self-discipline required for self-improvement.

4. *We learn to prejudge from early conditioning.* Most of us learn our prejudices from parents, early influences, friends, and social circles. In some parts of the country, prejudice runs strong. The jokes, comments, and

slanderous ideas regarding ethnic superiority, gender deficiencies, and socioeconomic differences are tempting to believe and at times ever more tempting to perpetuate.

When kids hear their parents put down other people, they assume this is normal and proper. It takes only one generation to make a behavior or attitude extinct, good or bad. The reason why we still have such bastions of prejudice in America is that parents keep teaching their kids to buy into these ideas. They do this because they learned them from their parents, who bought into the same misperceptions. Most of this modeling is unintentional, everyday, knee-jerk. No one intentionally sets out to be a bigot.

Most of us would not think of ourselves as the redneck stereotype, but we make snide remarks about preachers, laymen, bosses, politicians, Republicans, Democrats, doctors, lawyers, police officers, teachers, the old, looks-deficient people, the mentally slow, blonds, women, men, teens, and on and on. And if we were honest about it, we'd admit that we're showing our prejudice.

"But you're taking the fun out of life," some may say. True, much of our humor is at the expense of other people. We often hide our prejudices in humor to make them socially acceptable, but the toxin is still ingested. Once we buy into these ideas, it is difficult to ignore them and not pass them on to our kids.

Becoming Your Own Best Ally

Recognize Your Current Bump Signs

What are the bump signs that you've erected in your life? How do you excuse your attitudes and behaviors with past influences, temperament, and wiring? Certainly we all have negative characteristics, but when we use these characteristics to legitimize our insensitivity, weaknesses, and unloving behaviors, we defeat ourselves. One way to discern your possible bump signs is to make a list of everything that best describes you:

- Ethnicity and nationality (Jewish, Hispanic, African American, white, etc.)
- Religion (Catholic, Jewish, Muslim, Mormon, Buddhist, Baptist, charismatic, Presbyterian, Nazarene, etc.)
- Birth order
- Family life and early history
- Temperament (choleric, phlegmatic, melancholy, sanguine, or any other favorite terms)
- Pet peeves
- Negative past experiences
- Family income
- Relationship with dad, mom, brothers, sisters
- Physical assets—what would you change about yourself physically if you could?
- Unique characteristics that make you an individual (A.D.D., always late, messy, obsessive/compulsive, homosexual, alcoholic, suffering from migraines, high strung, anal, diabetic, having high blood pressure, sugar deficient, etc.)

You may realize that you've used such a list to explain why you are the way you are. These can be cheap ways to help others cut you slack without your having to carry the burden of getting better. All of us have different "crosses to bear," requiring varying degrees of effort. Recognizing how you may be using labels to avoid the real work of growth is a first step toward taking down your bump signs.

Remove Bump Signs

The Iowa road crew could not fix all the potholes and road bumps at one time. They had to prioritize them and work down the list. Once you've identified what signs you may have erected, pick one or two that you want to work on specifically. If you're gutsy, ask a friend or family member to hold you accountable in that specific area. Just as they say possession is nine-tenths of the law, in this case awareness is nine-tenths of the solution. Coming to terms with the self-descriptions you're hiding behind is sometimes enough to reduce this behavitude.

Work at Not Labeling Others

To a certain degree all of us depend on prejudging to know how to relate to people, avoid being harmed by them, and better communicate. If we had to do significant background checks, interviews, and personality testing with every person we meet prior to interacting with him or her, our social circles would be extremely limited. But the use of assumptions, both good and bad, is risky. It can produce cold wars, hate crimes, and verbal if not physical assaults.

What are your prejudices? What people groups do you favor? What people groups are you biased against? If you state none, then chances are you are not in tune with yourself, because we all possess a certain degree of prejudice. How can you go out of your way to get to know a person who falls within a group that you do not like or trust? Have you been disappointed by people in the groups you are biased against? What do you learn about people and about yourself in the process of analyzing your prejudices?

Pay the Price

There is no way around it—growth takes work. For the road department to send out a crew, redirect traffic, cut into the concrete, fill in the hole under the road, and patch the concrete, time, money, and energy must be expended. The road crew may have to put up with adverse weather and the risk of being struck by cars passing. But the only way to fix the pothole is to go out and do it.

Every pothole in our character requires effort to recognize and fix it. The easy way out is to put up a bump sign and ignore it. After a few months, you don't even see the sign anymore, but the risk of damage and disaster is real. By posting the sign, you think you've covered the bases and assume no responsibility for the injuries the bump creates. You say things such as, "That's your problem." "You don't have to work here." "You didn't have to marry me." "You knew that when you went into business with me." Sometimes, people start making excuses for us. "That's just the way Dad is." "You have to cut Mom some slack." "Joe can't help himself." "Jill is just difficult to work around." When people put up with our bump signs, they do us and themselves a disservice because we never get better. Often we get worse. Do what it takes to fix the pothole, even if the pain and cost are significant.

SELF-SABOTAGE ASSESSMENT

Place a value of 1 to 5 in the box beside each statement: 1 = no/rarely 2 = infrequently 3 = sometimes 4 = usually 5 = yes/always

☐ 1. I refuse to participate in prejudicial statements about others, serious or joking.

☐ 2. I try to behave in a way that is loving and kind, regardless of how others treat me.

☐ 3. I avoid bump signs or "that's the way I am" statements to excuse myself.

☐ 4. I am aware that I use labels to describe myself and explain my actions and attitudes.

☐ 5. When apologizing, I try to say I'm sorry without disclaimers or explanations.

Add the numbers and divide by 5. If your score is 1–2.5, you are probably being an enemy to yourself in this area. If your score is 2.6–3.75, you may want to consider this area more to see what is fuzzy or what you could do to improve it. If your score is over 3.75, you are either strong in this area or partially blind, which may require a perspective of someone who knows you well.

Self-sabotage assessment: _____

Another person's assessment of me: _____

UNPACKING PROCEDURES

1. How have you seen people use bump signs to license their weaknesses and lack of manners? What are the specifics and why do you think people resort to these labels?

2. How have you seen people's prejudices affect their behavitudes toward others?

3. What are some possible bump signs you have erected in the past or present?

4. What can you do to become aware of and remove present bump signs?
5. What can you do to avoid prejudging people and to withhold judgment until getting to know them better as individuals?
6. What is the difference between recognizing or labeling a characteristic and hiding behind it as an excuse for what we lack in life? How should we warn people of our idiosyncrasies without pre-determining and licensing our actions?

Seventeen

SCAB-PICKING

You know, I would have made it in business if it weren't for my dad. He made no attempt to help me get going. He's a wealthy guy, but he had the idea that we kids needed to make it on our own without any outside help. He said that if we had it in us, we'd amount to something. So he spent it all on himself and his companies, and then finally gave it to some nonprofits, which probably didn't need it. Definitely they didn't need it as much as I did.

You know why most businesses fail? They are undercapitalized. I had a plan to make it big, but I just could not raise sufficient capital. I had too many bills stacking up, too many creditors banging on my door. So I pulled the plug. All the time, Dad could have easily helped me succeed if he had not been so focused on himself. Well, maybe some day I'll make it, but it won't be thanks to any help from him.

Description and Dangers

Sometimes children are intrigued by the healing process after a scratch or scrape. The body produces a dark, hard substance commonly referred to as a scab. Children, because of their curiosity or dislike of the scab, are tempted to pick at it, perhaps even pulling it off. When they do this, they interrupt the healing process and open themselves up to infection and scarring. That's why moms tell their kids, "Don't pick at your scab. Let it heal."

As a child, my wife always wanted to break a leg or an arm so that she could get a cast and all the attention a cast produces. For all of us, war wounds, old sports injuries, and scars from surgery can be badges of honor. They can serve as medals of valor, because we faced something difficult, looked fear in the eye, and were victorious.

Today, casts come in all sorts of colors, which really attract attention. When my youngest son broke his arm a few weeks ago, he didn't want the pink, blue, or green designer options. He chose basic white. He wanted to remain inconspicuous, low-key.

Unlike my son, a lot of people take pleasure in showing their scars and talking about their wounds. Once wounds are healed, they get far less attention. After my son had his cast taken off, no one came up and asked him how his arm was doing. The same is true of our emotional wounds. An emotional cast, scab, or oozing wound attracts attention from others. We pick the scab to keep the wound from healing and thereby gain ongoing attention from others.

Do you have the following symptoms of seeking the sympathy of others?

1. You frequently talk about past hurts you've experienced.
2. You perpetuate problems by procrastination, creating new conflicts, and finding new ways of avoiding closure.
3. You don't forgive others and often talk about the ways they have grieved you.

The Danger of Preventing Healing

One danger of this behavitude is that we never heal. Walking through life as a wounded person is neither enjoyable nor productive, yet we become fixated on some of the benefits that come only from open wounds.

Many people get stuck at the point where they are wounded. A dramatic illustration of this is in the movie *Forrest Gump*. Forrest saved his commanding officer in a war zone, but only after the officer had lost both of his legs in an explosion. For years, his commander lived a bitter life, blaming Gump for saving him. Later in life, he healed from the loss, even though, of course, he never got his legs back. The point is that even though we may not be able to reverse our loss, we can heal from it. But replaying the loss and picking at the emotional scab prevents healing.

I heard one counselor say that when a child experiences the loss of a parent through divorce, often the child will get stuck at that stage of emotional development. He or she grows older chronologically but remains emotionally immature, continuing to struggle with the same issues as at the time of loss. They are all around us, people whose wounds have debilitated them. They walk with a limp and hurt people around them as they growl their discontent. When you add a few walking wounded to a family or any social setting, it will put relationships in jeopardy, paralyze team spirit, and interfere with productivity.

The Danger of Avoiding Responsibility

By picking our scab, we avoid the healing balm that comes when we extend ourselves in love to others. If we get better, we won't get the same attention. We may think we'll evaporate into the background; we'll be ignored.

This kind of selfish attitude overflows into an unwillingness to help others. Because we're preoccupied with our own wounds, we frankly have no time or energy to concentrate on healing others. This is self-defeating in that we overlook significant fulfillment and a sense of destiny by focusing too much attention on ourselves. The person who is willing to heal and avoid scab-picking is healthy enough to attend to the needs of others.

When we keep our wounds open, we may feel free from the burden of being responsible, but avoiding responsibility is selfish. Like a lazy factory worker, we fake our illness so as not to be forced back onto the assembly line. If we can moan loudly and show enough blood, we may be listed on the disabled sheet and forever be overlooked for hard labor. At first, this seems like a bonus. But after a while, being left out results in loneliness and isolation. We are lumped together with those who are permanently disabled. The number of people on the emotional welfare line, who delay their healing through scab-picking, creates a burden for the rest and takes care away from those with legitimate reasons for being on the line.

The Danger of Not Progressing

Scab-picking is a way of staying where we are in life. The engine is on and the tires are spinning, but we're going nowhere. We place ourselves in a holding pattern. Perhaps our motivation is fear of the future, anxiety about leaving a comfort zone, and insecurity about moving forward. There is a neurotic quality about perpetuating our problems. Some call it a loser's limp. If you watch a football player running down the field, only to fall by tripping over a teammate, sometimes he'll get up and limp off the field. By feigning injury, he let's everyone know that there was a reason for his failure that had nothing to do with clumsiness or incompetence. His limp is an attempt to gain mercy from potential critics. "See, if I hadn't hurt myself, I could have crossed the goal line. I was on my way when this terrible, unfortunate event happened to me. Poor me. I am hurt."

The Danger of Gaining Sympathy but Losing Respect

While an immediate goal of scab-picking is the sympathy we gain, it doesn't take long for that sympathy to evolve into disrespect. All attention is not the same. It can put us in the limelight, so we feel noticed, but this kind of attention can eventually backfire because along the way people lose respect for us.

Right or wrong, wounded people are often treated like broken tools, overlooked for promotion, leadership, raises, best-friend status, and other roles where respect is required. Leadership studies show us that popularity at all costs can actually work against leaders. If we complain and tell our woes as a way to gain influence, we will rarely be viewed as leaders. For that matter, healthy people will tend to avoid us as friends, even though they may offer us help.

By perpetuating our wounds, we are often perceived as needy, weak, and immature, which in turn works against our gaining respect from others. By confusing the attention we gain through sympathy with respect, we undermine ourselves. People no longer put their trust in us in the way they may have otherwise.

Perpetuating Our Wounds

Why do we pick our scabs when it is self-defeating? Here are four reasons:

1. *We are love-deprived and find sympathy through telling our sad story.* Love empathizes with people in need, but empathy is not necessarily healthy love. When someone feels sorry for us, mourns with us, or extends sympathy, he or she loves us based on our needs and not our strengths. Because the person's love was generated by our wounds, we foster our hurts so as not to lose that love. A person with an

empty love bucket is apt to use what is available to harvest love. If being wounded causes people to be sympathetic toward us, we are motivated to stay wounded.

While it is a demeaning concept, the truth is that the scab-picker is basically an emotional beggar. Manipulating empathy from people becomes a way of life. Instead of gaining love through healthy means, this person shows people his or her wounds, just as a panhandler might do in a Third World country or on an inner city street. Hustling compassion continues because of the power of reinforcement. When we find something that works, the behavior is reinforced.

2. *We confuse receiving sympathy with self-worth.* When our sense of worth is externally based, we are forever searching for affirmation and attention from others. While the sympathy we receive is not necessarily affirmation, we gladly substitute it for attention that boosts our self-esteem. All of us like to be attended to when we've been a victim or unfairly treated. That's why public relations people understand that a dissatisfied customer will tell seven to twelve friends, and a satisfied one will tell only two to four.

When we get attention, we associate that with worth. People would not spend their time listening to us if we didn't matter. Therefore, to affirm our value and existence, we tell others how we've been done wrong. "The police shouldn't have pulled me over." "The waiter treated me so lousy." "The pastor was so inattentive to my needs." "My spouse did me wrong." "My kids don't respect me." "The boss treats me like dirt." "My employees constantly let me down." "Circumstances (luck, God, fate) have really been unfair to me." The boo hoo list seems endless, but behind what may be valid wounds is a need for personhood validity and self-esteem.

When our self-esteem is low, we rely on external means of support. To avoid the risk of ending this stream of attention, we perpetuate old wounds or create a series of new ones that will garner more sympathy from well-wishers. In essence, we become mini–pity-party addicts.

3. *It's easier to walk with a cane than to go through physical therapy.* The main reason we indulge in self-defeating behavior is because it is less work for us in the short run. The same is true of this behavitude. When we rely on other people to carry us emotionally, it is easy to develop an unhealthy dependency on them. While we never intended to walk with a cane forever after our injury, it just seemed to be the easiest thing to do. Instead of going through the rigors of physical therapy, we decided to use a cane, which has the benefit of attracting attention. While there are many people who have physical problems and genuinely need the aid of medical equipment, there are many who use emotional neck braces, walkers, and designated parking places because using them takes less effort than getting better.

Working through the healing process can be painful and it rarely happens without effort. While personal growth is more difficult for some than for others, everyone needs a certain level of maturity and energy to accomplish it. If we lack energy or fail to develop maturity, we run the risk of being swept away by the currents of self-pity.

4. *We're afraid that people will forget the hurts we've endured and/or those who have hurt us.* While we talked about forgiveness in a previous behavitude, our unwillingness to forgive can also be seen in the scab-picking behavitude. One way to keep people who have

wronged us in a negative light is to show others the wounds that they've caused.

In *The Scarlet Letter*, the woman who committed adultery was forced to always wear the letter "A" on her clothes so that everyone would know of her sin. Long after the act had been committed and potentially forgiven, the embarrassment endured. By keeping our wounds from healing, it is as if we post pictures of the people who wounded us on the Post Office wall so that everyone can see how terrible they are. We fear that, if we don't keep reminding people of what happened to us, they will forget, so we keep the past crime as present tense to defame the depraved soul who did us wrong. Seeking revenge, we act as a judge in punishing the person who has hurt us. We can't forgive because that would mean letting the wound heal.

Becoming Your Own Best Ally

Be Serious about Healing

"Do you want to be healed?" This was Jesus' question to the paralyzed man at the Bethesda pool in John 5. This may be the most difficult question you'll answer, because an honest response can force you to confront self-defeating attitudes and behaviors. Growing up is hard to do.

The problem with many of us is that we are dishonest with ourselves. We are embarrassed to admit that we are keeping our wounds open. "Obviously I want to be healed. Why do you think I come down here to this healing pool every day unless it is to be able to walk again?" The question must be asked, even if it seems rhetorical and insensitive. We cannot assume that we really want to be healed because we have much to gain in retaining our handicapped parking pass.

The demand to go back to work, forgive, and progress with life seems at times overwhelming. "What if people forget about the jerks that offended me? Who is going to warn others unless I continually tell people how I've been wronged?" If you say, "Yes, I want to be healed," you must then answer the question, "How much do you want to be healed?" If you're really motivated, it will require picking up your mat and walking. You run the risk of humiliation if you try and fail. You may need to give up on some of your fellow cripples. But if you're serious, healing is within reach.

Find True Friends

As we noted previously, a co-dependent is someone who actually gains emotional fulfillment by associating with a person who is unhealthy. This aiding and abetting nature appears to be love but it has more to do with a parasitical relationship, each taking advantage of the other's weakness for personal satisfaction.

When you have someone who loves you but who is not willing to let you get away with self-destructive scab-picking, you have a true friend. When someone will say to you, "Grow up; get over it; let it go," without walking away from you in disgust, you have the right person in your life. We all need people who will sympathize with us, but sometimes we need a kick in the rear more than a pat on the back. Both are required for us to mature. The temptation is to seek out those who will sympathize with us and encourage our scab-picking. In fact scab-picking clubs exist where members gather for the sole purpose of telling each other how hard they have it and how they've been done wrong. This pity party becomes a mosh pit of pain but rarely motivates the participants to heal. Healthy friendships enhance healing, like a good salve on an abrasion.

Get Your Attention off Yourself

Since the motivation for scab-picking behavior is to get others to look at you, a remedy is to focus your attention on others. How can you find someone who needs a helping hand? They are all around you. Perhaps the hand is sympathy; perhaps it is tough love. Listening instead of talking, telling stories that affirm other people, and getting busy with wounded people are ways to get over your own pains. While you're investing in other people, you are being healed.

We are not designed to function best when absorbing attention from others. We were created to love, give, and get out of ourselves. By focusing on your own pain, you tend to become overly focused on yourself, which in turn makes the pain seem worse. Busying yourself with helping others distracts you from your own hurts.

When my kids begin complaining about not having the latest toy or clothing label, I know it's time to take them to feed the homeless at the Phoenix Rescue Mission or down to Mexico to work in an orphanage. The old saying is true, "I was singing the blues, because I had no shoes, 'til out on the street, I met a man with no feet."

Use Your Past Wound to Help Heal Others

There is nothing that will help you in your ability to heal others as much as having gone through similar wounds yourself. No one relates to someone in pain more than a person who has been through comparable pain. Counseling is difficult when we have not experienced what another person has gone through. Whether it is rape, losing a child, divorce, drug addiction, cancer, death of a loved one, bankruptcy, betrayal, or failure, the best person to provide meaningful support and encouragement is someone who has experienced the same thing.

Great healing can come from your wounds, if you are willing to let it. This healing is not just for other people. You will grow as well by helping others heal. When you refuse to do this, you leave work undone. God has a way of using our hurts to help heal others. He is great at re-cycling—turning garbage into something useful. When the wounded help heal others, it is akin to receiving a transfusion from someone who has developed the anti-body to a snake bite or disease. In addition, wounded heal-ers receive benefit as they help others because they take their focus off themselves.

SELF-SABOTAGE ASSESSMENT

Place a value of 1 to 5 in the box beside each state-ment: 1 = no/rarely 2 = infrequently 3 = sometimes 4 = usually 5 = yes/always

1	1. I avoid talking about past hurts.
1	2. I am able to forgive and not talk about people who have hurt me.
3	3. I have people around me who will lovingly hold me accountable for licking my wounds.
2	4. I have helped people by sharing with them from my past wounds and experiences.
1	5. I rarely talk about situations when I have had bad experiences or people who have let me down.

Add the numbers and divide by 5. If your score is 1–2.5, you are probably being an enemy to yourself in this area. If your score is 2.6–3.75, you may want to consider this area more to see what is fuzzy or what

you could do to improve it. If your score is over 3.75, you are either strong in this area or partially blind, which may require a perspective of someone who knows you well.

Self-sabotage assessment: _____

Another person's assessment of me: _____

UNPACKING PROCEDURES

1. What are your most painful past hurts or wounds?
2. Do you feel as though you have healed from them?
3. What can you do to help others in similar situations?
4. Do you know of someone who is a scab-picker, who seems fixated on a past wound?
5. Can you think of someone who has gone through a major hurt or trauma who seems to have healed well? What is the difference you note between the scab-picker and the person who has healed?
6. Why do we feel uncomfortable forgiving people after they have hurt us? How do people avoid letting others off the hook for hurting them?

Eighteen

NAVEL-GAZING

Lately, it's been getting worse. Jan's starting to drive me nuts. All she talks about is herself. "My car, my kids, my house, my vacation, my golfing, my clothes, my hair." If I have to listen to another hour of how her husband just doesn't listen to or understand her, I'll go crazy. Can't she see that she drives people away?

I know she's got a busy social calendar, but I don't think she has many friends. How could she? No one can get a word in edgewise. I'm very tempted to tell her what I think, but I'm sure she'd just write me off like the people she tells me about. I don't want to hurt her, because I think she considers me one of her best friends, but I wish she could think of someone else once in a while.

Description and Dangers

Our society could be characterized by expressions like "looking out for number one," "winning by intimidation," "do what seems right to you," and countless other phrases that describe our self-centered orientation. Obviously we cannot not be disinterested in our own health and vitality or we would be suicidal. But when does our self-focus cross the line into an unhealthy self-preoccupation? When do we self-indulge to the point of alienating others, causing our relationships to dwindle, and reducing our lives to tiny islands?

Copernicus was ostracized for his revelation that the sun does not revolve around the earth. A part of personal growth is accepting the reality that the world does not revolve around us, in spite of our feelings of dominance and prominence. With a twist in our motives, our gifts, time, and treasures become self-serving tools that destroy others. Listen to any group of people and you can hear them talking about the same person—I. "That's interesting, but I . . ." "I don't know about you, but I . . ." "I . . ." "I . . ." "Do you know what I did today?" "Here's what I think. . . ." The irony of navel-gazing is that we become so focused on ourselves that it ends up causing us harm.

Do you have the following symptoms of being focused on yourself?

1. You do most of the talking in conversations and/or are easily bored when others talk.
2. You frequently get into conflicts, small or large.
3. You donate less than 5 percent of your time and money to agencies outside of your work and/or your direct benefit.

The Danger of Alienating Others

Because people by nature are predominately self-focused, we tend to avoid others who are not able to concentrate on us. The irony is that self-centered people strive to get attention, but alienate people because of their inability or unwillingness to get beyond themselves and into others. That is why there are so many lonely souls in a world burgeoning with more than six billion people.

We create psychological islands when we focus on "me," which turns off potential friends and associates. Most people have very few real friends, regardless of how busy their social calendar is or how thick their address book. The problem is that self-focus does not grant us the time or energy to know, care for, or maintain our relationships because being a true friend takes time and energy.

Sometimes you'll hear self-focused people gathering in huddles. There is practically no dialogue, just various monologues, sometimes even overlapping each other. Listening has become a lost art. We think it is merely waiting for our turn to talk, and there is nothing as irritating as having someone tell you his or her story when you want to tell yours.

The other morning as I was working at the coffee shop, I overheard one woman talk for nearly thirty minutes straight about the details of a rendezvous she'd had the night before. Her friend barely uttered more than a few sentences the entire time. I wondered how the two women would respond if I asked them, "Is this person your good friend?" I imagine that the one talking would say yes and the one listening would say maybe. People get turned off by navel-gazers.

The Danger of Being Unfulfilled

Another downside of this self-defeating behavitude is that we end up overlooking what we're striving to find. Most navel-gazers are on a mission. Their borderline-obsessive trek leads them down the path of self-preoccupation. Regardless of whether you are a talker or not, too much mental concern about you and your needs will tend to keep you from what you seek most, fulfillment. The road to self-discovery eventually takes us out of ourselves, which is the only way we will find meaning in life. When we get stuck on the "me" freeway, missing the off-ramps to "youville," we are bound for a destination that creates little enjoyment or significance. "But many who are first will be last, and many who are last will be first" (Matt. 19:30). "The greatest among you will be your servant. For whoever exalts himself will be humbled, and whoever humbles himself will be exalted" (Matt. 23:11–12).

Just as the self-righteous never consider themselves proud, the self-centered are blind to their preoccupation. With rare exceptions, the less self-focused we become, the more aware we are of our self-centeredness. By looking inside for answers, we usually fail to find them, because the process is flawed, not necessarily the goals. The people of Israel wandered in the wilderness for forty years because of their unwillingness to get out of themselves and trust God. Today many wander internal wildernesses. Their preoccupation with finding themselves within themselves goes unfulfilled. There's a difference between soul-searching and navel-gazing. The soul-searcher seeks out inner problems to identify for growth. The navel-gazer looks within for solutions, but is frustrated and usually ends up finding more problems on the outside.

The Danger of Being Too Introspective

Balance is required for healthy living. A person who never looks inward is apt to be out of touch with his or her strengths and weaknesses, and probably is not a growth-oriented person. But when we spend an inordinate amount of time thinking about what we want, our goals, our blockages, and what others think about us, our perceptions are apt to be skewed as well. Right now, hold this book 1 to 2 inches from your eyes. Go ahead. What did you see? Just a lot of dark, fuzzy lines. Your ability to comprehend what you read requires that the book be back far enough for your eyes to focus and scan the words. When we get too close to or too far from ourselves, or any problem for that matter, we will lose our perspective. What we see will be distorted—too close and we'll exaggerate the significance of what we see; too far away and we'll underestimate the importance of a matter. With such distortion, we will be unable to make appropriate choices.

The Danger of Not Enjoying Others

Wise is the person who discovers that the greatest goal in life is not happiness. We have certainly overestimated that ideal in America. But many of us confuse happiness with peace, fulfillment, and joy. The latter are by-products of finding significance through helping people. No matter how task-oriented we are, we need relationships to help us grow and discover things outside of ourselves. At times this means helping others by using our gifts and resources. At other times it requires letting others help us. And always we need the joy of simply having friends, peers, and equals to walk with through life.

When we navel-gaze, we spend too much time and energy on ourselves and too little on others. As a result, we actually lose touch with ourselves because a part of us will experience atrophy without healthy interaction with other people. Healthy interaction is not just letting others enjoy our presence. Shallow social relationships do not provide the joy that comes from actually making a difference in people's lives. To be fulfilled requires us to get outside of ourselves.

Focusing on Ourselves

Why are we self-centered when it is self-defeating? Here are four reasons:

1. *We've been taken advantage of by others.* Ouch. When people take advantage of us, it makes us want to pull into ourselves and not trust others. "I won't let them

do that to me again. Fool me once, shame on you; fool me twice, shame on me!" It takes only a couple times of someone pulling the chair out from under us for laughs, for us to begin looking around and hanging onto the seat as we sit. While paranoia is unhealthy, people usually hover between trust and paranoia, especially among unproven friends. Since each of us is the only one truly looking out for number one, it is only natural to become self-focused.

When past experiences of trust have resulted in embarrassment, hurt, and feeling betrayed, our instincts tell us to keep others at a distance for our own security. Even if we avoid becoming overtly cynical and jaded, we still are careful to retain a pleasantly polite distance from others, an invisible moat just in case marauders try to pillage our personhood.

2. *Nothing gets our attention like our inner pain.* Self-centeredness is not just a by-product of insecurities. Pain gets our attention. Just as physical pain is nature's way of telling us something is wrong with our body, emotional pain lets us know there's an internal problem. When we have been hurt, we are naturally inclined to pull inward and look at ourselves. That is why some of the most introspective people you meet are folks who have experienced pain in their past.

Events in our lives that cause pain distract us and slow down our ability to interact in other areas of life. It's like having a migraine. I'm told that the pain gets so bad, you almost cannot function. Every ounce of energy goes toward basic maintenance, because the pain is so distracting. Or it's like a traffic accident in the opposing lane. Traffic in your lane slows down because the drivers are rubbernecking, distracted by what's happening in the other lane. Self-engaged people nearly always have past or present emotional pain that distracts them to the point of taking their attention off others and focusing wholly on themselves.

3. *We underestimate the rewards of getting outside of ourselves.* Self-indulgence isn't all it's cracked up to be. While channel surfing, I'll occasionally breeze through MTV. I've watched enough of it to hear quite a few testimonials from partyers around the world, suggesting that there is nothing like a hedonistic romp on the town.

Self-indulgence, while offering the potential for extreme short-term pleasure, never produces real joy and often leads to disaster over the long haul. Drunken dancing and drug bingeing are as self-centered activities as you'll find anywhere. Just the nature of a one-night stand precludes any long-term pleasure for anyone. Though we are told by the media's marketing and advertising that self-indulgence is the way to go, we eventually find that preoccupation with self is shallow and unfulfilling.

On the other hand, the benefits of getting beyond ourselves are quite exhilarating. Our perspective improves. We attract friends and find fulfillment in seeing our attention improve the lives of others. Our attitude toward life is healthier, because we find answers beyond ourselves. By finding our purpose through serving others, we function more as we were created to function.

4. *We've been taught that the answers lie within us.* When my car is acting up, I take it to a mechanic whom I trust to tell me the truth and to fix it without adding any inflated charges. I know that the car, being a car, cannot fix itself. The difference between motor vehicles and humans is that the humans are under the impression that they *can* fix what ails them, that the answer lies within them.

If you plant a melon seed that produces fruit, you can trace each melon back to a vine that is rooted in the ground. The fruit is not the vine or roots, but it is what gets most of our attention. Traditionally teachers of Christianity have focused their attention on our negative fruit, such as adultery, lying, stealing, murder, gluttony, and attitudes like greed, lust, hate, and anger. If you follow the vine, you'll find a common root, the sin of trying to be our own god, to run our lives in spite of what God says, and in essence to compete with his divinity. According to the Bible, it is the problem, not the solution, that lies within us. We must look to our God for answers to our inside problems.

Becoming Your Own Best Ally

Satisfy the Craving

Since we ended the problem section with a description of sin, it is only natural to begin the solution section with the antidote to sin. We all have cravings. Some are physical, sexual, mental, emotional, as well as spiritual. At the core of every person is a soul, the source of spirituality that defines who we are more than our looks, IQ, or personality define us. When our soul is hungry, we become self-absorbed and often try to fill it with things that do not satisfy. We often fill our soul hole with things like shopping, new cars, sex, thrill entertainment, plastic surgery, food, limelight, new jobs, and drugs. The physical equivalent is junk food bingeing when we're stressed or hungry late at night.

To satisfy the craving within, we must recognize soul hunger for what it is and feed our souls with that which is spiritual and healthy. This may or may not be church. Soul food should not be confused with empty traditions, just as it is not the list of junk food items we just listed. As a student of human nature and spiritual nutrition, I have found that the most effective craving satisfier is a personal relationship with your Maker through Christ, as described in the Bible.

Get Counseling

I remember as a kid, sometimes my shoes would be so tightly knotted that I had to ask Mom or Dad to untie them. As adults, sometimes we get so tightly wound around ourselves that we have to ask for some help in untangling our knots. That is the role of the counselor. I believe in counseling but not in all counselors. Just because a person is licensed or has a Ph.D. after his name does not mean his advice is worth a hill of beans. Smart people are not always wise people. Counselors are human too, and they have mortgages and car payments. When you pay someone to help you get to the point where you won't need him or her anymore, there is a potential conflict of interest. I say that not to belittle professional counselors but to help you understand the requirements for finding a good counselor.

Before you decide on a counselor, interview the counselor and find out where his or her expertise lies, what he or she charges, and any other pertinent questions you have. Make sure there is moral and philosophical compatibility. While you're not marrying him or her, you want to make sure the counselor does not lower your standards. When you undergo counseling, you should be able to see some measurable progress within ninety days. While healing for serious issues will take longer, no progress sensed within three months is a good indicator that you may not have found a good match in your counselor. While some counselors may argue with that advice, my experience tells me that this is a good rule of thumb.

Seek help, but remember that all help is not the same. Effective counseling aims to keep a person from becoming dependent on the counselor-client relationship and from becoming overly self-focused. Because the process of counseling can actually induce you to become self-focused as you look inside and try to untie some of the knots, you need to guard against staying in that condition for long, lest you become a professional navel-gazer.

Help Someone Else

I've coined the word *behavitude* because it expresses the strong link between attitude and behavior. Sometimes attitude comes first and produces action and other times action begets attitude. A strong example of the latter is the power of helping someone less fortunate than you. By feeding the homeless, doing a good deed anonymously, and pouring yourself into someone else, you have less time and energy to focus on yourself. You can get caught up in helping others so that you actually forget about the problem or goals that have consumed you. In fact one of the prescriptions for combating common depression is to actively help someone.

Being a true servant, however, is being a person with a serving heart, not just a person who does servile acts. We've all had waiters who took our order and brought us food, but who did not exhibit an attitude of service. Merely helping people to help them is a start, but it does not guarantee you'll develop the right attitude. At the same time, you cannot have a servant's heart without demonstrating it tangibly through acts of service. The servant attitude emerges as you learn to get out of yourself, surrender control of your life, and elevate the inherent value in others.

Tithe Your Time and Money

There is an incredible therapeutic effect in tithing your time and money to help others. While the concept is biblical in nature, established to provide 10 percent of one's income for God's work and funding his mission, the benefits of tithing have been grossly overemphasized in terms of funding church budgets. As a pastor, I am very well aware of the need for money to run a church, just as any businessperson understands the role of economics in running his or her organization. But I'm also especially aware of how nervous people are about money issues and the negative stereotypes of money-hungry clergy that abound. Many of these stereotypes are founded on a few well-publicized scandals, along with hearsay conversations.

I think the major reason people are so defensive about money talk is that it has a lot to do with our desire for control; money is power. We exchange our lives for money, which in turn can provide so many of the things we need in life. Most of us in America don't have to pray, "Give us this day our daily bread," because we know that if push comes to shove, we can provide our own bread for a number of days to come. People lie, steal, cheat, and kill for money. Why? Because it is power, which ties it closely to our souls. As we give our time and money to help others, we relinquish some of our desire for unhealthy control and power.

SELF-SABOTAGE ASSESSMENT

Place a value of 1 to 5 in the box beside each statement: 1 = no/rarely 2 = infrequently 3 = sometimes 4 = usually 5 = yes/always

☐ 1. I give more than 5 percent of my time and money to causes not directly related to my work or family.

☐ 2. I avoid dominating conversations or talking a lot about myself.

☐ 3. I listen well to others and ask them questions about themselves.

☐ 4. If you were to ask other people, they would say I tend to be others-oriented and unselfish.

☐ 5. I know a number of people well because I've taken time to listen.

Add the numbers and divide by 5. If your score is 1–2.5, you are probably being an enemy to yourself in this area. If your score is 2.6–3.75, you may want to consider this area more to see what is fuzzy or what you could do to improve it. If your score is over 3.75, you are either strong in this area or partially blind, which may require a perspective of someone who knows you well.

Self-sabotage assessment: _____

Another person's assessment of me: _____

―――

UNPACKING PROCEDURES

1. Why do you think people get so self-centered?
2. How can you tell that someone is self-centered?
3. What shows you that someone is not self-centered?

4. How do you pursue your goals and focus on personal growth without getting out of balance and being preoccupied with self?

5. What can you do right now to be more others-oriented?

6. If you're gutsy, ask a circle of your friends or associates how you are in terms of listening and showing interest in them. You may want them to answer anonymously if you want reliable feedback.

7. What do you think about the suggested spiritual solution of seeking the answer outside of you—God—for the problem inside of you—being your own god?

Nineteen

THAT'S JUST THE WAY THINGS ARE

"Pastor, there is no way I can overcome these things in my life. I have to face the facts. I'm divorced and things are not going to get better."

"Why do you say that? Don't you believe that God can do something new in your life?"

"You know, life just seems to work differently for me. Other people live happily ever after, but I've always had a more difficult time in life."

"So what does faith have to do with it?"

"What do you mean?"

"Faith is that decision to see what is invisible and to live as if there is a God who can do incredible things in your life."

"I'm just not a risk-taker. I have resolved to be satisfied with my lot in life. Things are never going to change. That's okay."

"It sounds like you're giving up."

"Well, I'm not giving up on life. I'm just giving up believing that things are going to ever get better, that I'm going to find Prince Charming who will put me on his horse and go riding into the sunset. I have to live the life I was given. I have to settle for that."

Description and Dangers

Fatalism sees things as they are, reducing life to a series of unavoidable events and circumstances. There is very limited room for creativity, faith, or risk-taking. This is the Missouri syndrome, "The Show Me State," where we limit our lives to what we can see instead of what can be.

Some people have a very difficult time seeing what can be, while others venture expectantly into the domain of possibilities. The inability or unwillingness to see things as they could become is a debilitating behavitude, keeping us locked in today and yesterday. Rarely do we see tomorrow for our lack of faith. Not seeing the possibilities in opportunities, relationships, or our own personal growth keeps us locked into limited living. We justify our lack of faith that things can change by pointing to what is currently visible, assuming that others, who bank on what is invisible, are behaving irresponsibly. We think something is wrong when they seem to recognize a reality that is not measured by the five senses.

I intentionally saved this behavitude for last, because if you're prone to fatalism, you will be tempted to employ this with any of the previous behavitudes to explain why you can't or won't improve. I want to leave you with the idea that your life can significantly get better, internally if not externally, or both.

Do you have the following symptoms of fatalism?

1. You live life according to what is visible, rarely venturing out on faith.
2. You avoid the risk of the unknown and thus start few new ventures.
3. You base your future on what is versus what can be.

The Danger of Missing Out on a Big Part of Life

Scientists tell us that the human eye is able to pick up only a narrow spectrum of energy waves. The human ear has a limited range of audio waves that it can hear. Dogs and other animals can hear things we assume do not exist, simply because we have no natural equipment to verify them. It is both naive and quite prideful to assume that reality is defined merely by what we are able to measure.

Even if we admit there are horizons beyond our recognition but do not venture beyond what we can see and touch, we lose out on a big part of life. Columbus would never have discovered the Americas had he not pushed away from the shore and charted toward the edge of the earth. Men would not have set foot on the moon had they not dared to do what was inconceivable a few years earlier. Every great discovery that has become a part of our everyday lives—TV, telephone, cell phones, computers, cars, airplanes, microwaves, medicines, and the Internet—were one day considered ridiculous because they lay outside the boundaries of what was known. There is a vast space that exists beyond what is now tangible to us. When we pretend that the only reality is what we've experienced, we limit what we will ever incorporate into our lives.

The Danger of Diminishing Our World

The result of faith avoidance is that our lives will tend to be small. I'm not talking only about technological possibilities. When we avoid living with the invisible, the world of possibilities, we exist with a reduced emotional, relational, and spiritual capacity.

Our new congregation was looking for land for a permanent home. Because most people have a difficult time imagining what can be, we had an exhibit in our lobby of a possible property master plan. Churches have measured the tangible impact this makes. Once people are able to visualize the walls, stucco, parking lot, and address, even though their senses say they do not yet exist, capital donations improve significantly. If you want to live in a world without ambiguity, you will have to be self-incarcerated in a tiny cell. Living without faith windows creates a gloomy (internal) environment.

The Danger of Not Helping Others Live by Faith

Because a majority of people depend on others for a large number of their cues in life, we underestimate the importance of our role in living by faith. A part of our purpose in life is to encourage the faith in others who have relegated themselves to clutching the guardrail on the ship of life. By modeling faith, we can help them realize that progress is ahead of them, not behind or under them, that they have to go out on a limb to pick fruit, and that life without risks is a contradiction. We must live boldly, daring to plow new ground, even if it is only in our own garden. By living toward our potential, pursuing a life of what can be versus what is, we unofficially become cheerleaders for others, encouraging them with the idea that if we can do it, they can do it too. Our life is not just about ourselves. It's about serving others and influencing them by the way we live.

The Danger of Becoming Cynical

"I have half a mind to . . ." is a major problem in life; there are far too many half minds. "I'm fat; that's just the way I am." "I'm insecure." "I'm not creative." "I've blown it in my marriage." "I'm not very talented." "I'm lazy." "I don't know enough to do something else." The world is full of justifications for our lack of faith living, but the results are nearly all the same. We grow into cynical people.

Pascal, the French philosopher and mathematician, asked this question about his faith in God: "If I'm wrong and there is no God, what have I lost? But if the unbeliever is wrong and there is a God after all is said and done, what has he lost?" The risk of missing out on what can be is huge. First Corinthians states that the three greatest life traits are faith, hope, and love. The elements of this trilogy interact with each other over and over. Hope helps us be positively motivated and optimistic. Love makes us appealing to be around. And people who lack faith ultimately diminish their hope and love.

A Lack of Faith Living

Why do we limit our reality and our lives to only what is observable? Here are four reasons:

1. *We've never been taught to believe, to exercise faith.* If we have witnessed very few acts of faith, we have a difficult time understanding the concept. We base much of our belief system on what we have experienced. If we grow up around people who lived within the five senses and rarely ventured beyond what was predictable or already existing, we may find it difficult to live by faith.

   I meet a lot of people who grew up going to church but who quit when they left home. The main reason is that they did not see that religion made a big difference in the lives of their parents. They attended scores of church services with little lasting impact. Sometimes people with no church background are better prepared to live by faith than those who thought they were living by faith simply because they attended a church. I'm sure you've heard that going to church does not make you a Christian any more than driving into a garage makes you a car. Church attendance works against faith when it injects you with such a small dose that you become inoculated against the real thing. Find a congregation where people of faith gather to fan the flames of belief, not just perpetuate the cold coals of yesterday's cookout.

2. *We have been conditioned by the scientific notion that reality is only what can be proved in a laboratory.* What makes this so intimidating is that many scientists are very logical and have high IQs. We assume by their degrees and white lab coats that they know more than we do. So when they attack our faith with statistics, theorems, and requests for findings from our studies, we feel at a loss to defend what we believe. While all of this sounds antiscientific and irresponsible, it is quite the opposite. Scientific methodology can prove and even predict certain things, but it is limited. Responsible scientists admit the limitations of any given study and methodology.

My point here is that some truth transcends scientific provability. In the movie *Contact,* a very skeptical scientist is asked to prove the love between her and her father. She realized that some things in life lie beyond scientific definition.

3. *We confuse fiction with nonfiction yet to be.* History has proved that what others previously considered fiction, for example, flying, landing on the moon, cars, and radio waves, was just preexistent reality. To suggest something does not exist or is not possible may simply be admitting that you don't know about it or how to accomplish it right now. In Bible times the most reliable way to detect false prophets was by waiting to see if their prophecies came true. When

they did not, a foreteller was considered a false prophet and thrown out of camp.

A baby still in the womb is nonfiction yet to be perceived. Technology has allowed us to know when women are pregnant within just a few days after conception. In the past, we had to rely on intuition, missed periods, morning sickness, and an eventual protruding midsection. Though all of these are indicators of the presence of a baby, the ultimate proof of pregnancy is when the baby is born. Now, with ultrasounds and monitor printouts, we can actually see the life within the mother before we can hold it. But even before that life can be seen, if a woman has conceived, she is pregnant, just as pregnant at one month as at nine months. Those who can accept it on faith, believe it though there are no outward signs. Others won't believe it until they see the evidence of a protruding abdomen. Dreamers understand that dreams are conceptions, pregnant ideas that are under development and will be eventually birthed unless we abort them.

4. *Our self-image is based on the opinions of others who don't believe what they don't see.* Let's use pregnancy as a word picture again. If a woman is four or five months pregnant, it usually isn't obvious whether she is indeed pregnant or just gaining weight. More than once I've made the embarrassing mistake of asking a woman, "So, when are you due?" The response is, "I'm not pregnant!" Oops! At a certain point, because she can't fit into her normal clothes and to squelch the rumors, a pregnant woman begins wearing maternity clothing to remove doubt about her discipline at the dinner table. Then at eight or nine months, complete strangers put their hands on a pregnant woman's stomach, asking, "When are you due? Is it a boy or girl? Your first?"

Does a woman base her pregnancy on the responses of these people? Of course not. She knows whether or not she's pregnant, regardless of what people say. So why is it that we take our cues about what is reality and what can become reality from strangers, or worse, well-meaning friends who may have little idea as to the gestation period of our dream or goal?

The most dangerous person in the world may be a negative-thinking expert. Because of the individual's education, title, role, or experience, he can disseminate all kinds of pessimistic pollution with a credibility that makes it stick. When our self-esteem is not secure and when we tend to rely on external sources for our self-image, we are susceptible to the negative opinions of others and to giving up on our potential because of what someone said.

Becoming Your Own Best Ally

Get Faith

Nearly every observable reality was at one time an unobservable possibility. Faith is the heart's ability to see what is currently unobservable and to act toward what is possible. In many cases, faith is the key that unlocks the possibilities within a situation. I could walk up the street to any number of houses on my block and not be able to enter, because I do not have a key to them. I therefore could not (without breaking the law) experience the inside of the home. I'm forever restricted to driving by on the outside—unless someone has a key and invites me in. This is how most people experience life. They wait for those with the keys of faith to first unlock the possibilities. Then they walk through the already opened door. The point is that you don't merely have to watch others implement their faith. You can have your own set of keys. Read on to find out how.

Nourish Your Mind

Garbage in; garbage out. Your mind can work only with what it is fed. The impact of a positive, motivational book or audiotape is hard to beat. We all need our batteries recharged on a regular basis. Peale, Schuller, Waitley, Ziglar, Maxwell, Lucado, and similar authors are gifted in helping us look at the possibilities in life when our natural temptation is to focus on the negative. Keep at least one inspirational book going at all times.

Some of the most faith-filled literature available is within the Bible. Outside of John 3:16, the most practical sentence in the Bible is Philippians 4:8: "Whatever is true, whatever is noble, whatever is right, whatever is pure, whatever is lovely, whatever is admirable—if anything is excellent or praiseworthy—think about such things." This attitude-conditioning program contains the elements that build our faith muscle and keep our attitudes functioning effectively. *Truth* has to do with what is real, versus gossip, innuendo, and hearsay. Cognitive therapy focuses on telling yourself the truth. *Noble* refers to royalty. Think like a king. Don't stoop to common thoughts. *Right* thinking has to do with ethics, integrity. Our thoughts both reflect our soul's condition and influence it. *Pure* is all that is spiritually uplifting, free of moral filth and mental pollution. *Lovely* includes what is beautiful and the best in people, versus what is ugly. *Admirable* can describe the things that prudent, wise, and disciplined people whom you look up to think and say. *Excellent* has to do with quality control, monitoring what goes in and what comes out. Total quality management is about attitudes, not just corporate effectiveness. *Praiseworthy* describes the good news, not the bad. Search out the positive word to say; overlook the bad. These eight, great guidelines are what I refer to as *faithinking*, connecting faith to our thinking and attitudes and thus affecting our behavior.

Hang Out with Positive People of Faith

If you are what you eat, you become how you think, and eventually behave like those you hang around with most. The world is full of naysayers, people who project their own inner negativity onto others. Why let your faith be tempered by the doubts of others? Life is too short to spend time with people who are geared toward small thinking and expectations limited to what was or is. Obviously, you may be married to this person or be forced to spend large chunks of time with him or her. If not, do what you can to avoid voluntary time with faithless others. If so, make sure you supplement your schedule with time around positive people. This can make all the difference in your attitude, especially if you have a propensity to let others' comments affect you.

While there are certainly exceptions, I have found on the average a more positive attitude and higher faith level among active church attendees than among inactive. Certainly you can find something positive and negative in nearly every person and situation. The fact that a person discovers one over the other is a matter of attitude and disposition far more than of more firmly grasping reality. Regardless of the situation, there are positive ways of looking at and dealing with the dangers and challenges. You don't have to be naive, gullible, or blind to display faith. To discover a person with a positive attitude, look for trends in his or her behavior. Attitudes, whether of faith or faithlessness, prevail over time.

Try Something New

What does your soul want to pursue that is not already visible or tangible? What could you do today that would cause you to live by faith? I'm not talking about some irresponsible, hair-brained idea, but one that has merits, even though yet unseen. This is what I call *responsible irresponsibility.* We need to break out of the box, concentrate on a dream, goal, or nonfiction yet to be. The possibilities that arise from *faithinking* are significant. Most people live lives that require little to no faith, outside of taking on extra debt on their credit cards. Future goals require faith, so long as we cannot guarantee the results. Many people view good planning as having all the details figured out beforehand. That sort of thinking does not require faith and rarely accomplishes anything significant. Goals that inspire us and others are those that involve plans but are primarily faith-oriented. If we pursue the goals, we will have to believe with our souls not just our heads. The ability to inspire another person with our faith walk is an added benefit of living this way. Our faith endows others with the courage to also live by faith.

SELF-SABOTAGE ASSESSMENT

Place a value of 1 to 5 in the box beside each statement: 1 = no/rarely 2 = infrequently 3 = sometimes 4 = usually 5 = yes/always

☐ 1. I step out on faith consistently.
☐ 2. I avoid being significantly influenced by other people's concerns or doubts.

☐ 3. I base my goals on what is possible, not what is sure.

☐ 4. I am able to see the possibilities in people and situations and myself.

☐ 5. I tend to verbalize what is positive and hang out with optimistic people.

Add the numbers and divide by 5. If your score is 1–2.5, you are probably being an enemy to yourself in this area. If your score is 2.6–3.75, you may want to consider this area more to see what is fuzzy or what you could do to improve it. If your score is over 3.75, you are either strong in this area or partially blind, which may require a perspective of someone who knows you well.

Self-sabotage assessment: _____

Another person's assessment of me: _____

UNPACKING PROCEDURES

1. Why do you think so many people are tempted to focus on what is here and now instead of seeing the possibilities?
2. Think of someone you know who has the ability to apply faith to everyday life. What helps him or her live this way?
3. Think of someone you know who is fearful and who tends to live according to what is tangible instead of seeing what can be. What is the result of this attitude?

4. When in the past have you stepped out on faith and failed? What did you learn from this experience?
5. When have you taken a risk that paid off? What did you learn from this experience?
6. What is your biggest challenge among the eight *faithinking* guidelines taken from Philippians 4:8? Why?
7. How can you increase the amount of faith you exercise in living out the principles you've learned in this book and pursue what you can become instead of what you are already?

LAST BUT NOT LEAST THOUGHTS

Wow! Congratulations! You've finished this book. Yippee! Yee haw! Hug yourself. Pat yourself on the back. Kiss your reflection in the mirror. High five yourself. You've shown a lot of moxie to continue reading to the end. To have gotten this far probably means you've wrestled inner alligators and may have even flirted with some depression. Looking at ourselves in the mirror of self-defeating behavitudes is not necessarily a warm, fuzzy process. But if you've made it this far, chances are you have faced some less than pretty things about yourself, all on the road to beautiful. You are to be commended. And if for any reason you feel intimidated by the work left to do, know that your awareness of self-sabotaging behavitudes is the biggest single step because behavitudes are so elusive. They are tough to see and own in ourselves. Finding them in others is much easier!

The only downside of getting this far is the danger of what we might call the self-defeating behavitude of head knowledge. People who grasp a concept intellectually sometimes assume they've conquered it. The Bible says,

Do not merely listen to the word, and so deceive your-selves. Do what it says. Anyone who listens to the word but does not do what it says is like a man who looks at his face in a mirror and, after looking at himself, goes away and immediately forgets what he looks like.

James 1:22–24

Just as going to the grocery store and filling your pantry with food are different from preparing dinner and eating it, so is reading a book different from applying it.

Life and people are very complex. Obviously a list of the nineteen most common ways we defeat ourselves will not encompass all our shortcomings. While most authorities point to such things as childhood trauma, lack of self-esteem, dysfunctional family life, and an array of predispositions to weakness to explain why people don't reach their potential, my focus has been on more subtle erroneous zones.

Many in my field of work oversimplify the role of spirituality in the context of sin and our relationship with God. "If you get right with God," they claim, "everything will work out just fine." While spirituality is a vital part of understanding how life is intended to function, we must be wary of too simplistic solutions.

In this book, we have acknowledged that there are few black and white solutions to the tendency of some toward self-defeat, but some effective antidotes have emerged. After years of listening to the woes of people and how they ended up in their place in life, both good and bad, I see certain patterns. Because living is not a hard and fast science, my approach has been more of a sage, subjective summary, based on many scenarios.

We all have stories or dramas in which we are actors. But the essence of *My Own Worst Enemy* is that we are also often the playwright and director. We are more involved in our failure than most of us want to admit, and less the cause of our successes than we like to claim.

If you have not found any of these nineteen self-defeating behavitudes familiar, perhaps it is that your behavitudes lie among the potentially hundreds of hybrids I have not had space to discuss. Of course, it could also be that you have some blind spots, closets where you have tucked away your private stash of excuses. After all, that's the underlying danger of these self-sabotaging conditions—it's difficult to see our role in them.

I trust you'll find hope in coming to grips with the responsibility you carry. Certainly more than pat answers, pop psychology, or theology, the power of these concepts comes in confronting the ways we defeat ourselves. The chest-pounding, finger-pointing, foot-stomping that goes on as we pass the buck for our failures is nonproductive. Because we can control neither the actions and behaviors of others nor circumstances, we do best to focus on what we can control—our own behavior. By looking for the enemy outside ourselves, we shirk the burden of the possibility that we are our own worst foe.

Imagine what life would be like if everyone worked on just these nineteen behavitudes. But for now, forget the world or society at large. What if your family and close friends began to seriously take responsibility for themselves and addressed these behavitudes? What a wonderful world it would be. Yet enjoying being around others who are more mature is not our main goal. Sharing the benefits of our own growth with others is the primary objective.

Emotional and spiritual maturity are certainly not automatic results of chronological age. There are some pretty immature old people and middle-agers, still wearing emotional diapers. Don't be fooled by the cars in their garage, fancy degrees on their office walls, or poised demeanor. They may still have a lot of maturing to do. Some of us have more barriers than others to overcome, but we all have hurdles. No one is exempt.

Comparing your insides with others' outsides is a dangerous thing to do, because we can easily become demotivated. Most of us have little idea of where a person is in his or her journey, what inner battles he or she fights, or from where he or she has journeyed. Giving up the fight is not an option for you. By "tending to our own knitting" as grandma used to say, we stand a better chance of personal growth, which of course turns us outward as opposed to inward.

Life needs more cheerleaders, people who will applaud and encourage us. The more you cheerlead, the better your chances of being cheered on and of being encouraged by your own words. When you feel like giving up, ease up a bit but don't quit. Lace your running shoes and go another round. Eventually you'll begin to enjoy the fruit of your investment of work and struggle.

Remember that life is not a me-do-it project. Self-help courses have their limitations. If all the power we need were truly within us, we would not see so much struggling around us. The idea that I can do it alone sells well in the marketplace, but the results are dismal. Our Creator wants us to understand that we can be our very best only when we surrender our best and worst to him. Nurturing this most important relationship will take us farther toward realizing our potential than any single practice.

I'll never forget April 1995 when I was assigned to the notification team in the Oklahoma City bombing tragedy. I was one of several counselors and pastors who assisted on the fourth floor of the Christian Church. When one of the 168 victims had been positively identified, the family was called to the fourth floor, where they would first officially hear those dreaded words, "Your loved one is dead." Watching the people as they heard the bad news and being available for support and consolation helped me see up close the horror of the crime that had been committed.

Six years later, I was intrigued to observe the process by which Timothy McVeigh prepared for his execution. By issuing the well-known poem "Invictus" by William Ernest Henley as his last statement, McVeigh seemed to be both taking responsibility for and defiantly embracing his crime.

The intent of Henley's words, "I am the master of my fate; I am the captain of my soul," was to motivate readers who, like the poet, face very intimidating circumstances. He was encouraging us to persevere, not to surrender to self-doubt and fear. For McVeigh the statements are true within limits. He was not the captain of his soul to the end. The judicial system was. We are masters—small *m*—and captains—small *c*. Ultimately all of us will have to give an account to our Maker and he will decide our eternal fate. If we are captains of our souls, he is Commander in Chief.

Because God has given us free will, we have the ability to select our fate within limits. Right or wrong, good or bad, God gives us enough rope to lasso success (defined as maturity and fulfillment) or to hang ourselves. Free will is both a tool to liberate us and a device to incarcerate us, depending on how we use it. Regardless, the responsibility is our burden to bear. Blaming others and circumstances for the majority of our problems is a way of relinquishing our power and deceiving ourselves. We've been blessed. We must use our gift wisely. That is the point underlying *My Own Worst Enemy*. When we limit our potential, we miss out on many wonderful things in life.

My hope and prayer are that you and I use this incredible gift of free will for our own good. Life is too short to waste it, too long to endure its misuse. Thanks for letting me be your coach and tour guide through these messy issues. If you have been encouraged by these words, I look forward to hearing from you, so that I can be encouraged on my path as well.

Assessment Overview

If you compare your self-assessment results with those of others, you may not have a true indication of how you stand. The results are more a revelation of how hard or soft you were on yourself compared to others. Consistently low scores are indicative of low self-esteem; you were too hard on yourself. Conversely, scores that are too high may show that you overestimated yourself, allowing pride to deceive you. Better than comparing your scores with someone else's, look at all of your self-assessment scores and then focus on the four to six self-defeating behavitudes that are causing you the most trouble. Below is a list of the nineteen behavitudes we have discussed. Write in the average self-assessment score you computed at the end of each chapter and circle four to six that have the lowest scores. These are the ones to attend to first.

1. _____ Spilled Milk—guilt
2. _____ I Can't Say Yes—unwilling to commit
3. _____ Show-and-Tell—materialism
4. _____ Puppet People—letting others control you
5. _____ He'll/She'll Make Me Happy—depending on others for happiness
6. _____ Investing in Junk Bonds—wrong priorities
7. _____ Hung by the Tongue—what we say
8. _____ I Can't Say No—lack of discipline
9. _____ Have Bags, Will Travel—running from problems
10. _____ Look, Mom, No Hands—living to please others
11. _____ Stone-Throwing, Gnat-Straining, Camel-Swallowing, Speck-Picking, Plank-Avoiding Behavitudes—being critical

12. _____ Run and Hide—running from the truth
13. _____ Buried Treasure—avoiding your dreams
14. _____ Looking Back—living in the past
15. _____ Quick and Easy—compromising for speed and
        ease
16. _____ Bump Signs—labels and excuses
17. _____ Scab-Picking—keeping wounds from healing
18. _____ Navel-Gazing—self-centeredness
19. _____ That's Just the Way Things Are—fatalism and
        pessimism concerning possibilities

Alan Nelson, who has a graduate degree in psychology/communication and a doctorate in leadership from the University of San Diego, is founding and senior pastor of Scottsdale Family Church. He is a popular speaker, trainer, author, and columnist for *Rev.* magazine. Alan lives in Arizona with his wife of twenty years, Nancy, and their three sons, Jeff, Josh, and Jesse.

Contact Alan at www.LeadingIdeas.org